Joseph Henderson

Prophets I Have Known

The author with President Heber J. Grant at the railroad station. This scene was repeated frequently during nearly two decades.

Joseph Anderson Shares Life's Experiences

Prophets I Have Known

JOSEPH ANDERSON

Published by
Deseret Book Company
1973

ISBN Number 0-87747-508-3
Library of Congress Number 73-88327

Lithographed by

DESERET PRESS

in the United States of America

PREFACE

My service with the brethren of the First Presidency and the other General Authorities of The Church of Jesus Christ of Latter-day Saints has been a very unusual and rewarding experience. It has provided the opportunity and privilege to study these men, to witness the guiding hand of the Lord in the leadership of the Church in a way that perhaps few, if any, others could do.

For many years I have been urged by my family and numerous friends to write my experiences in the office of the First Presidency. I have been reluctant to do so, being convinced that my associations with these remarkable men and the work of the Church which is entrusted to them are of such a confidential and sacred character that it would not be wise nor advisable to make them public.

I feared that were I to publish them I might betray confidences, which would be something entirely contrary to my life's training and desire.

However, after much thought and repeated persuasion by certain brethren of the General Authorities that such a contribution would strengthen the faith of our people and increase testimonies to the truths of the gospel, I have responded. I have been persuaded that perhaps a worthy purpose could be served by a personal account of some things that have transpired and so impressed me in my long service as secretary to the president of the Church and to the First Presidency.

After half a century of such association I can say the men who have presided over this church from the beginning have been raised up by the Lord for the particular time during which they served. They have been and are men prepared and well qualified for the service they were to render and the leadership they were to give. They have never been mediocre men. Instead they were and are giants of the Lord, chosen and ordained before they came to this earth to perform the work assigned to them.

Fortunately they are not of the same mold. Each differed from the others, but all, however, were highly spiritual, men of revelation, of devotion, and of faith. They have been and are prophets of the living God.

Some years ago a prominent business executive said that the greatest asset of a man or a nation is faith. He said:

"The men who built this country and those who made it prosper in its darkest days were men whose faith in its future was unshakable. Men of courage, they dared to go forward despite all hazards; men of vision, they always looked forward, never backward. In these days of stress, let us hold to faith, faith in divine leadership." (Thomas J. Watson)

Whenever the gospel has been upon the earth, the Lord has had prophets and representatives through whom he has made known his will. Through them he has given commandments to his people. When they have hearkened to the counsel and word of the Lord they have been blessed. When they have rejected his word, destruction has come upon them. Such has been the case since the beginning of time.

The Lord loves his children and wants to bless them. He knows what is for their best good, and accordingly, he has made these things known through his servants, the living prophets.

It has been a thrilling and very humbling experience over a period of 50 years to have association with five presidents of the Church, with 13 combinations of brethren serving in the First Presidency, and with 46 apostles, and the many other General Authorities of the Church. It has been a rare assignment to meet with the First Presidency nearly every morning and with the First Presidency and the Twelve every Thursday in their meetings in the Holy Temple. There have been, as well, many other occasions to feel of their spirit and to know of their devotion and integrity.

It has been a blessed and inspiring privilege to have the love and confidence of these brethren and to have the responsibility of keeping a record of their meetings.

Space will not permit my discussing each of the brethren I have associated with over these many years. My failure to do so is by no means a suggestion that their influence upon me and upon the Church has not been as impressive as that of those who are mentioned herein. On the contrary, the brethren who, during my time, have served as General Authorities have had and now have my utmost confidence, love, and esteem. I have refrained from mentioning in this record the brethren of the Twelve who have passed away and those who are now serving. I have a deep affection for each of them and any association with them is stamped indelibly upon my heart. To attempt to write my impressions of these great and noble men would require volumes. Accordingly, it is advisable to draw a line of limitation.

In quoting rather extensively from some of the brethren to whom I refer, it is with the thought in mind that few of the young people now living have heard of or read some of these faith-promoting and inspirational incidents. The hope is that the older generation who may have heard them will find interest and testimony enlargement in refreshing their memories. Some of them are taken from shorthand notes that heretofore have not been transcribed.

I perhaps have referred to past administrations more than the present. This has been done in the thought that there are living at the present, few, if any, who can give the firsthand account that I can of these events and that the experiences related should not be lost to future generations. The all-important present is built upon the sturdy foundation of the past, as the glorious future will in turn have a close relationship both to the present and the past.

ACKNOWLEDGMENTS

Producing a book involves the skills of many people, and I am deeply indebted to many individuals for their encouragement and help.

For many years I have been associated with the board of directors and the management of Deseret Book Company as its secretary-treasurer. Because of this closeness, I had not ever thought I would write a book myself, but after much persuasion and encouragement from the board and others, I felt to undertake the project. I am grateful that they were persuasive enough to bring me to the task.

I am especially appreciative of the editorial assistance given to me by Henry A. Smith, press secretary to the First Presidency. His efforts have been invaluable in the final writing and editing of the material.

I also want to express love and gratitude to my beloved companion, Norma, and to members of my family who have been great motivators in getting me to record the events of half a century spent with spiritual giants of the Lord.

Most of all I am grateful for the brethren whom I have had the privilege to serve. I acknowledge their spiritual greatness, and will be indebted to them forever for the examples of righteousness they have been to me. Life has been full and satisfying for me because of such associations.

Joseph Anderson

CONTENTS

SECTION FIVE

SECTION SIX

1

I Start My Life's Work

February 1, 1922, was a most important—indeed a red-letter—day in my life. As I look back to that day it is difficult to realize that it was over a half century ago. Yet, I realize so much has happened within the Lord's earthly kingdom; there has been so much of progress, with significant events bringing with them so much of interest and so many happy, inspiring experiences, it seems improbable that they could be crowded into the space of only 50 years.

It was on that day, after several interviews, that I began to work as the secretary to the president of The Church of Jesus Christ of Latter-day Saints. Little did I realize at the time what supreme joys and responsibilities lay ahead of me.

I was excited but humbled and a bit frightened when I first met with President Heber J. Grant. It would be putting it mildly, indeed, to say that I was awed just to be in the presence of that great man. He spoke with an honest, sincere frankness and was so kind and friendly that he completely won me over. That day was the beginning of an association of mutual love and confidence that was to last more than two decades.

As secretary to the president I first worked alongside George F. Gibbs, who was the secretary to the

1

First Presidency. It was not until October 1923, a year and a half later, that I became also secretary to the First Presidency and began meeting weekly in the Salt Lake Temple to record the minutes of those sacred and inspiring council meetings of the presidency and Council of the Twelve.

Right from the beginning I was fearful of the responsibility of taking those minutes, organizing and condensing them, and then reading them back the next week for approval of the brethren. I have always been appreciative of their frequently offered resolutions of appreciation. As the years passed I gained more and more confidence, overcoming my fears, but never ceasing to be awed in the presence of these great men.

President Grant's counselors at the time of my earliest association were Charles W. Penrose, who was then nearing his ninetieth birthday, and Anthony W. Ivins, who lived one of the most colorful careers of any of the General Authorities I have ever known.

Perhaps as I list the names of the members of the Council of the Twelve I first met with, the reader will recognize names that are now legendary in their accomplishments and the legacy they left for us of their generation. Seated in their order of seniority in a circle in the temple council room, they were:

Rudger Clawson, President of the Twelve, and Elders Reed Smoot, George Albert Smith, George F. Richards, Orson F. Whitney, David O. McKay, Joseph Fielding Smith, James E. Talmage, Stephen L Richards, Richard R. Lyman, Melvin J. Ballard, and John A. Widtsoe.

This circle of Twelve Apostles was unchanged in its personnel for nearly a whole decade and was not broken until the death in May 1931 of Orson F. Whitney. The resulting vacancy was filled then by the appointment of Joseph F. Merrill.

Among these Twelve Apostles I first met with were

With one exception this picture represents the Council of the Twelve when the author began his service in 1922. Elder Joseph F. Merrill, was named to the Twelve in 1931, to fill vacancy occasioned by death of Elder Orson F. Whitney. Left to right: George F. Richards, Joseph F. Merrill, Joseph Fielding Smith, David O. McKay, James E. Talmage, Reed Smoot, President Rudger Clawson, George Albert Smith, Stephen L Richards, Richard R. Lyman and Melvin J. Ballard. Elder John A. Widtsoe, was in London presiding over the European Mission.

three who subsequently became presidents of the Church—George Albert Smith, David O. McKay, and Joseph Fielding Smith. The last one to pass away was Joseph Fielding Smith, who ended his career as the tenth president on July 2, 1972, only a few days from his ninety-sixth birthday.

As I approached my awesome duties, I was extremely conscious that in the beginning of the Church in 1830, the Lord told us through revelations to the Prophet Joseph Smith of the importance and necessity of keeping proper records. Surely the history of God's dealings with his people in the ages past emphasizes this need. The experience of Nephi in securing the Plates of Brass upon which were engraven the records of the Jews and a genealogy of his forefathers is an impressive example. The Book of Mormon itself is another outstanding illustration of inspired record keeping.

The account related in Third Nephi of Christ's appearance unto the Nephites and his interest in the records of that time has been a matter of much interest to me as an indication of the importance of proper records. There we read:

And it came to pass that he [the resurrected Lord] said unto Nephi: Bring forth the record which ye have kept.

And when Nephi had brought forth the records, and laid them before him, he cast his eyes upon them and said:

Verily I say unto you, I commanded my servant Samuel, the Lamanite, that he should testify unto this people, that at the day that the Father should glorify his name in me that there were many saints who should arise from the dead, and should appear unto many, and should minister unto them. And he said unto them: Was it not so?

And his disciples answered him and said: Yea, Lord, Samuel did prophesy according to thy words, and they were all fulfilled.

And Jesus said unto them: How be it that ye have not written this thing, that many saints did arise and appear unto many and did minister unto them?

And it came to pass that Nephi remembered that this thing had not been written.

And it came to pass that Jesus commanded that it should be written; therefore it was written according as he commanded. (3 Nephi 23:7-13.)

The Lord is working with the leaders of his Church today, as he had done during the past. Great things are happening in this Church; this is the dispensation of the fulness of times, and the Lord through his inspired leaders has chosen mighty men, good men, devoted and faithful men, men of the hour, to lead the affairs of his church in this day and time. They have the keys of authority, the keys of the kingdom, the keys and power of the priesthood.

It has been a glorious privilege to see the Spirit of the Lord working upon the leaders of his church, to be with them when they have prophesied in the name of the Lord and to see those prophecies fulfilled.

Sometimes we are inclined to accept the teachings, the inspiration, and revelations of the Prophet Joseph Smith and early presidents of the Church, but have some reservation in our minds regarding the decisions, advice, and counsel of our present leaders.

President Wilford Woodruff said on one occasion:

Now we may take the Bible, the Book of Mormon and the Doctrine & Covenants, and we may read them through, and every other revelation that has been given to us, and they would scarcely be sufficient to guide us 24 hours. We have only an outline of our duties written; we are to be guided by the living oracles. *(Journal of Discourses* 9:324.)

And I think that we would remember that President Woodruff also said:

I referred to the Doctrine & Covenants—a code of revelations which the Lord gave to Joseph Smith. This book contains some of the most glorious revelations upon doctrine, upon principle, upon government, upon the kingdom of God and the different glories, and upon a great many things which reach into the eternal words. . . . If we had before us every revelation which God ever gave to man; if we had the book of Enoch; if we had the untranslated plates before us in the English language; if we had the records of the Revelator St. John which are sealed up, and all other revelations, and they were piled up here a hundred feet high, the Church and Kingdom of God could not grow, in this or any other age of the world, without the living oracles of God. (*Millennial Star* 51:548.)

It has been aptly said that the Lord's will to Abraham did not suffice for the people of Moses' time; nor did the will of the Lord to Moses suffice for the people of Isaiah's time. The same could be said about the people of the Book of Mormon days. Different dispensations and different missions required different instruction; and that is true of the people of today. People become acquainted with the knowledge of the Father only as the Lord reveals it. Without the revelation of additional or new truth men would not progress in the world.

On another occasion President Woodruff said:

Read the life of Brigham Young and you can hardly find a revelation that he had wherein he said, "Thus saith the Lord," but the Holy Ghost was with him, he taught by inspiration and revelation, but with one exception he did not give those revelations in the form that Joseph did; for they were not written and given as revelations and commandments to the Church in the words and name of the Savior. Joseph said, "Thus saith the Lord" almost every day of his life in laying the foundation of this work. But those who have followed him had not deemed it always necessary to say "Thus saith the Lord," yet they have led the people by the power of the Holy Ghost; and if you want to know what that is, read the first six verses of the 68th Section of the Doctrine & Covenants, where the Lord told Orson Hyde and other to go out and preach the gospel to the people as they were moved upon by the Holy Ghost.

"And whatsoever they shall speak when moved upon by the Holy Ghost shall be scripture, shall be the will of the Lord, shall be the mind of the Lord, shall be the word of the Lord, shall be the voice of the Lord, and the power of God unto salvation." (D&C 68:4.)

It is by that power we have led Israel. By that power President Young presided over and led the Church. By the same power President John Taylor presided over and led the Church. [And I might interpolate here that it is by that power that his successors have led the Church.] And that is the way I have acted according to the best of my ability, in that capacity. I do not want the Latter-day Saints to understand that the Lord is not with us, and that he is not giving revelation to us; for he is giving us revelation, and will give us revelation until this scene is wound up. I have had some revelations of late, and very important ones to me. (*Millennial Star* 53:794-96.)

And then he mentioned the Manifesto pertaining to the discontinuing of the practice of plural marriage and said that the Lord had shown to him in vision and by revelation what would take place if we did not discontinue that practice. Some have questioned whether that was a revelation. We sometimes have such questions submitted to us now. President Woodruff said very definitely it was.

I can reaffirm the testimony of President Woodruff by bearing my certain witness that "by that same power" the presidents of the Church I have known have led the Saints of God.

This is a glorious dispensation in which we live—a dispensation into which all other dispensations of the gospel have been merged. Speaking of this dispensation and of the wonderful things that have happened, are happening, and will happen, and the fact that the Lord will pour out his Spirit upon all flesh, I have been greatly impressed by this quotation from the 121st section of the Doctrine and Covenants:

For there is a time appointed for every man, according as his works shall be.

God shall give unto you knowledge by his Holy Spirit, yea, by the unspeakable gift of the Holy Ghost, that has not been revealed since the world was until now;

Which our forefathers have awaited with anxious expectation to be revealed in the last times, which their minds were pointed to by the angels, as held in reserve for the fulness of their glory;

A time to come in the which nothing shall be withheld, whether there be one God or many gods, they shall be manifest.

All thrones and dominions, principalities and powers, shall be revealed and set forth upon all who have endured valiantly for the gospel of Jesus Christ.

And also, if there be bounds set to the heavens or to the seas, or to the dry land, or to the sun, moon, or stars—

All the times of their revolutions, all the appointed days, months, and years, and all the days of their days, months, and years, and all their glories, laws, and set times, shall be revealed in the days of the dispensation of the fulness of times—

According to that which was ordained in the midst of the Council of the Eternal God of all other gods before this world was, that should be reserved unto the finishing and the end thereof, when every man shall enter into his eternal presence and into his immortal rest. (D&C 121:25-32.)

This is a part of that great revelation that was given to the Prophet Joseph Smith on March 20, 1839, when he was confined as a prisoner in the jail at Liberty, Missouri.

We are seeing today a fulfillment of a part of that revelation in the remarkable accomplishment of placing men upon the moon and gaining information regarding that great celestial body.

These men who stand at the head of the Church are men of destiny. It is my firm conviction that they were chosen for their work before they came here.

I am convinced of the wisdom of the Lord in providing that there should be three men in the First Presidency. There is only one president at a time, and he has power and authority greater than any other living person. He is the mouth piece of the Lord; he has the last word. Whosoever sins he may remit, the Lord will remit. He has the keys of the sealing power, and he alone can delegate that power. He alone has the keys of authority to restore former blessings to one who has been excommunicated, and he alone can delegate that power. However, it is important that he have counselors to assist him and to counsel with; he may also call others to assist him in his work if he desires.

I have learned a great lesson in realizing that the Lord does not always whisper audibly to his servants, telling them what they should do in each situation.

They must figure things out in their minds, make a study of the situation, and seek the guidance and inspiration of the Lord. The Lord can and does, when occasion requires, make his mind and will known to his servants, as indicated by the Book of Mormon prophet Enos, who said, "And the voice of the Lord came into my mind, saying. . . . " If necessary the Lord can appear to his servants in person, as he did to Joseph Smith, but the Lord does not do such things to satisfy men's curiosity. It would seem that there would needs be some very weighty and important matter that would call for such a manifestation.

There is safety in such counsel, and it has been a glorious education to see the wonderful divinely inspired decisions that result from discussions of important matters that come before the First Presidency. I have marveled as each, a man of wonderful innate qualifications, expresses himself on the subject under consideration, and then how all three minds harmonize and reach the correct decision.

President George Q. Cannon, a counselor in the First Presidency during the administrations of Presidents Wilford Woodruff, Lorenzo Snow, and Joseph F. Smith, said, referring to the First Presidency:

There are at the head of this Church, chosen by the Lord, three men, who constitute what is called the First Presidency of the Church of Jesus Christ of Latter-day Saints. One is the President, the other two are his counselors. But all three are Presidents according to the revelations. One, however, holds the keys. President Woodruff is distinguished from every other one of us by the fact that he possesses the keys of the kingdom on the earth. He represents the supreme authority. His voice to us, in its place, brings to us the voice of God. Not that he is God; not that he is infallible. He is a fallible man. His counselors are fallible men. The First Presidency cannot claim individually or collectively infallibility. Infallibility is not given to men. They are fallible. But God is infallible, and when God speaks to the Church through him who holds the keys it is the word of the Lord to this people. Can President Woodruff do this without his coun-

selors: I do not know what he can do, or what he might do; but I
know that he does not do it. I know that President Young did not,
nor President Taylor. I know that President Smith did not. He
sought the counsel of his counselors. They acted in concert. And
when the First Presidency act in concert, they are a power.
But . . . if the First Presidency were divided, and the Twelve were
divided, then we would not have the blessings that God has
promised, and I do not know what would be our fate. (*Millennial
Star,* September 5, 1895.)

I can personally attest to the fact that the other
presidents I have known and worked with from President Grant down to and including President Harold B.
Lee have likewise sought the counsel of their counselors
and weighed it carefully before making decisions.

The question has occasionally been asked by
Latter-day Saints when the First Presidency has
issued a statement to the Church whether they were
setting forth their opinion or whether the Latter-day
Saints should accept the pronouncement as the word
of the Lord. In other words, would the members be
out of harmony with the Lord's will if they acted
contrary thereto.

Members of the Church, and others, have their
free agency to accept or reject the advice of the First
Presidency. There is no coercion. As stated by
President Cannon, individuals are fallible, but God is
infallible, and when these brethren unitedly give advice and counsel to the Church, whether it is over
their signatures or by oral expression, they are
speaking for the Lord. They are sustained by the members as prophets, seers, and revelators. Those who
think their understanding is better are at liberty to
act as they see fit, but they must accept full account-
ability for their actions.

It is as the late President Stephen L Richards
said:

When a judgment is reached and proclaimed by the Presidency
and the Twelve, it becomes binding upon all the members of the

Church. God's kingdom is a kingdom of law and order. He is a lawgiver and the Supreme Judge, but he has delegated authority and conferred the keys of the Kingdom upon these men whom he has chosen. They act for him . . . they act in response to the operation of the Spirit of the Lord.

It has been an inspiring experience to listen to the First Presidency discuss the many weighty problems that have arisen over the years. It is a rare privilege to hear the wise discussions and witness the inspired decisions where questions and problems are presented, and to be touched by the spirit of each as his feelings on the matter are expressed. It is thrilling to know his Spirit is directing the minds of his servants, and to have the Spirit bear witness to my own soul that the decision arrived at is in accordance with the will of the Lord.

These men, over the years, have been and are men with independent minds, men of faith, men with opinions of their own, men whose minds are not easily swayed. If Mormonism, so-called, were a false philosophy or church, it could not produce a group of men such as the General Authorities are and have been so far as my acquaintance with them over 50 years has shown.

These men are making scripture today. They are doing the will of the Father and his Beloved Son today as did the apostles of old. The disciples of the Lord when he was on the earth and following his departure left to future generations the gospel, spoken or written under inspiration. On occasion they gave their personal opinions on matters and so indicated. The same condition may on occasion prevail in our day. This does not detract from the truth that the Lord is at the helm, that there is a channel of communication, inspiration, revelation between him and his chosen servants—and that applies to local as well as general authorities, if they will conduct their lives prayerfully, devotedly, and unselfishly to the welfare of God's cause, seeking, studying, and serving.

I have often thought it must have been a great privilege to know the apostles of the Lord in the time of the Savior and subsequent to his resurrection—perhaps more so after the Lord left them, because they had the Comforter, the Holy Ghost, to be with them, the spirit of revelation attended them, and they enjoyed the gifts of the Spirit. They knew beyond any question that they were teaching and preaching the truth, the gospel of their Lord and Master, and they were willing to give their lives for that testimony.

I have concluded, however, that the same is true of the First Presidency and the Twelve today. They know they are special witnesses of the Lord; they know that the spirit of truth accompanies them and their utterances; they know that they are teaching the word of the Lord, and they are ready to give their all, including life itself, for the cause they represent.

SECTION ONE

Leadership of President Heber J. Grant

2

President Grant—A Man of Strength and Faith

I always looked upon President Heber J. Grant as an important and powerful link between the early pioneer prophets and leaders of The Church of Jesus Christ of Latter-day Saints and the more modern prophets even to this very day.

His parents were among the founding pioneers. In this new country, they, with others of the courageous and devout Saints, had struck roots deep into the soil of practicality and spirituality. Their extreme faith and the revelations of the true and living God in restoring gospel truths had illuminated their minds with an understanding of the purposes of life, of the pre-existence and eternal progression. These motivating forces—being a far cry from the false, stunted, and "pot-bound" ideas of their Christian contemporaries— had fortified them with the courage and determination to move beyond the reach of their enemies. They accepted and practiced a nobility of faith, hope, charity, industry, devotion to duty, and love of God and country. So strengthened, they bequeathed to their posterity these same fundamental principles.

Heber Jeddy Grant was born in Salt Lake City,

November 22, 1856. The pioneer Mormon community
was not yet a decade old when he was born a son of
its first mayor, Jedediah M. Grant, who also was a
counselor to Brigham Young in the First Presidency.
His mother was Rachel Ridgeway Ivins Grant, who
possessed an abundance of these sterling pioneer
qualities.

Mayor Grant died when his son was but eight days
old, and upon the mother fell the full responsibility of
rearing the child through her own toil and independence
and thrift. The son, in his later years, often "thanked
God for that mother of mine."

President Grant was called to the apostleship in
October 1882, just before his twenty-sixth birthday. His
call came as a result of direct revelation to President
John Taylor, who had succeeded Brigham Young as
the third president. Already the young apostle had
established himself as a Church leader. Two years earlier,
when appointed president of the Tooele Stake, he had
set aside personal ambitions and desires to devote himself to a career in business and finance at which he
would have made a remarkable success. Instead he was
foreordained to a life of church service and leadership
that was to bring him to the position of foremost importance in the restored church—prophet, seer, and
revelator and president of the High Priesthood.

One of his many interests was the Mutual Improvement Association, and in 1875 he became a member of
the Thirteenth Ward YMMIA superintendency, which
was the first ward to be so organized by Junius F. Wells
under direction of Brigham Young. This launched him
on a long career of MIA leadership, which included
becoming a member of the general superintendency and
business manager and one of the founders of the *Improvement Era.*

As an apostle, Heber J. Grant was assigned to open
up the Japanese Mission, and he remained in that land

for a year, returning to begin on January 1, 1904, an assignment as president of the European Mission, which at that time also included being president of the British Mission.

With this much of biography to introduce this wonderful man to the readers—realizing that many of you did not have the privilege of knowing him personally—I return again to my first statement of this chapter relative to President Grant's being an important link between the early prophets and the modern ones.

President Grant knew Brigham Young well since some of his closest boyhood associates were a son and a grandson of the pioneer president. President Grant often told of his experiences with Brigham Young and especially of running to the Lion House when the prayer bell rang and joining the Young family in the prayers offered by the father. Heber Grant was in his twentieth year when Brigham Young died. Many of the pioneer leaders, including his own mother, were close friends and associates of the Prophet Joseph Smith and his brother Hyrum—the martyrs who gave their lives for their testimonies in 1844.

It was John Taylor, Brigham Young's successor, who called President Grant to the apostleship. After that he had close and intimate association with three other presidents—five in all—before becoming president himself. These were Wilford Woodruff, Lorenzo Snow, and Joseph F. Smith. He also had had close comradeship during many years with those who followed him as presidents—George Albert Smith, David O. McKay, and Joseph Fielding Smith.

The link with our present-day prophet, President Harold B. Lee, is made complete with the realization that it was President Grant who in 1941 called President Lee to be an apostle and ordained him to this high office.

President Grant was truly a man without guile, and

he gave me the benefit of his utmost confidence. I kept all of his accounts. Every dollar that he received he turned over to me to pass through his accounts and place in the bank for him. He wanted to make absolutely certain that he paid a full tithing on every dollar that came into his hands. He trusted me implicitly, and I gave him no occasion to question my loyalty to him.

Loyalty is a two-way road. As an employee is expected to be loyal to his employer, so should the employer be loyal to the employee. President Grant fulfilled that requirement as completely and openly as any man could, and in return I would have given my life rather than be disloyal to him or take advantage of his confidence in me.

As secretary to the president, it became one of my duties to interview those who came to see him. It was not possible, nor is it possible or wise today, for the president of the Church to see everyone who calls or who would like to see him. There were many who had personal axes to grind, or chips on their shoulders. Some were interested in selling something and wanted to obtain the president's personal endorsements. Some came, I am sure, out of curiosity, and then there were the cranks, and some were charlatans.

It was important that the president see everyone whom he should see, and it was just as important that he not be bothered by those whose missions were not important or necessary. Within proper church organization it was then, as it is today, the policy that members with personal or doctrinal problems should take them to their bishops and stake presidents and that these authorities offer the solutions. When further help is needed then the local ward or stake leaders should take up the matters with the appropriate General Authorities.

As people came to the office, it required considerable wisdom and tact and, yes, often sought-for inspiration, to meet wisely every situation. There were those who had to be denied audience with the president, although an attempt was made always to make the refusal in the kindest way, and sometimes the individuals could be helped in some other manner.

Occasionally the person who had been thus refused managed to get the ear of the president in some other way. Some were unkind enough to say to President Grant, "Your secretary does not think I am good enough to see you." President Grant always manifested his loyalty to his secretary and his confidence in him by answering somewhat as follows: "That is what I have my secretary for, to take care of matters of that kind for me." Never did he take me to task for any decision I made in regard to these matters.

In September 1941 I wrote an article regarding President Grant and my feelings toward him at that time. When I wrote these words I had been his secretary for more than 20 years. As I have read over the things I said on that occasion, I find they are my feelings today. These written impressions have never left me, and I borrow from them today as the basis of my discussion in this chapter, since he passed away about four years after I wrote them.

On November 21, 1921, President Grant delivered an address in the Assembly Hall to the students of the Latter-day Saints University. He told of his experiences in overcoming obstacles and of his accomplishments through perseverance. To me this was an eventful day, for it was the first of his speeches that, at his invitation, I had attempted to report by shorthand. Upon my success that day depended very greatly the answer to my application for employment with the president of the Church. I shall always believe that he made it a special point to speak with the utmost rapidity on that occasion. Of one thing I am certain: it was with great difficulty that I followed him. On many occasions since then I had opportunity to learn just how fast President Grant could really talk.

That experience stands out so very vividly in my mind because it was the commencement of an intimate and enjoyable association with President Grant that endured for nearly a quarter of a century. As the years passed, my admiration and affection for him continually increased. One could not do otherwise than recognize his many virtues and profit by the wonderful examples he had set.

We should not seek for perfection in men—since no one is perfect—but no one who became intimately acquainted with President Grant could fail to recognize in him the fundamental human virtues of courage, loyalty, perseverance, generosity, initiative, faith, and *hard work*.

All his life he was an indomitable worker. He never felt that work hurt anyone. I am convinced that one of the qualities most responsible for his prodigious achievements was his love of work. Illustrative of his penchant for work is the fact that in his young manhood he toiled until the late hours of the night and into the early hours of the morning, devoting his dynamic energy to the tasks assigned to him and that he himself assumed. Surely hard work in his youth and young adulthood was one of the great foundation stones upon which he built the enduring ideals that went into the structure of the successful man.

During all the years that I knew him that same "drive" continued. Thousands of Latter-day Saints and many friends in the business world have received from him letters—long letters—dictated to the dictaphone late at night or in the early hours of the morning when he could not sleep. Many times when on a train going east or west, or perhaps away from home in a hotel room, he and I would be busy early in the morning—perhaps between six and seven o'clock—taking care of matters that needed his attention. Or perhaps he would send a message of comfort or cheer to 'someone whose heart was aching because of a tragic or distressing experience. Even when traveling by automobile to attend a conference in some distant stake he would often open the briefcase and answer correspondence or give instructions as to how certain matters should be disposed of. Not infrequently he remarked that he had never been able to catch up with his work. This he could never do, for he was always thinking of things to do to add to the happiness of others.

Nor did the situation change greatly whenever he was confined to his home because of illness. It was not unusual for him to take care of more work when he was ill than he did otherwise—this, of course, being due largely to the fact that he was then free from frequent interruption.

I recall the occasion when President Grant became seriously ill while in Los Angeles and on the advice of his physician was taken to the hospital. He was in a critical condition. Many friends sent flowers to cheer him and brighten his room; others sent letters of encouragement. Though almost too sick to talk, President Grant insisted that letters of thanks and appreciation be written to these friends, and he could not be dissuaded from signing these letters personally. It was with much difficulty that he signed his name, but he insisted on doing so.

President Grant had developed an attractive spencerian style of penmanship and took great pride in his signature, whether he was signing a letter or a memorandum or autographing a book. His personal calling cards were a reprint of his own signature.

There are many thousands of books today in the libraries of Latter-day Saint homes that bear this signature along with a personally inscribed friendly or affectionate greeting. The distribution of good books, without doubt hundreds of thousands of them in his lifetime, brought President Grant great pleasure. He felt he was doing this for the benefit and pleasure of the recipients, for he loved good books.

Thousands have been influenced to righteous living and noble thinking by the messages of the volumes he has given. Countless others have been comforted in times of trial or sorrow by reading his messages and accounts of his own experiences on similar occasions. I treasure beyond possible monetary value the dozen or more such books I have in my own personal library with messages and the signature of President Grant. Some of these are books by other authors; some are compilations of the writings, letters, and messages of President Grant. Some contain his favorite hymns, or especially loved poems.

One of these, a booklet he sent out for Christmas in 1939, contained a photograph of his mother with the following words of tribute:

I live today in the eighty-fourth year of my life as one whose mother was all to me. She set an example of integrity, of devotion and love, and of determination and honor second to none. Her life was a sermon that rings through my soul to this day. So near to the Lord would she get in her prayers that they were a wonderful inspiration to me from childhood to manhood. One of the main reasons I am President of the Church today is that I have followed the advice and counsel and the burning testimony of the divinity of the Lord Jesus Christ which came to me from my mother.

Often the pages in these Christmas booklets contained poems or messages in his own handwriting. One such, which he noted was copied into his notebook while in Japan in 1902, is so typical of his life and philosophy:

Luck and Laziness

Luck tapped upon a cottage door
A gentle, quiet tap;
And Laziness, who lounged within,
The cat upon his lap,
Stretched out his slippers to the fire

And gave a sleepy yawn;
"Oh, bother! Let him knock again!"
He said, but Luck was gone.

Luck tapped again, more kindly still,
Upon another door,
Where Industry was hard at work
Mending his cottage floor.
The door was opened wide at once;
"Come in!" the worker cried,
And Luck was taken by the hand
And fairly pulled inside.

He still is there a wondrous guest
From out whose magic hand
Fortune flows fast—but Laziness
Can never understand
How Industry found such a friend.
"Luck never comes my way!"
He sighs and quite forgets the knock
Upon his door that day.

—Author unknown

On yet another page are some statements by President Grant, really gems of thought revealing the wisdom, spirituality, and practicality that characterized his leadership:

Spoken by the Sender

(These sentences were selected by my daughters from some of my sermons and articles.)

There is nothing on this earth that brings so much satisfaction and comfort as the knowledge that we are in the line of duty.

*** ***

The Lord gives to many of us the still small voice of revelation. It comes as vividly and strongly as though it were with a great sound. It comes to each man according to his faithfulness, for guidance in matters that pertain to his own life.

*** ***

The average man is born with a capacity to stand on his tiptoes and reach out just as far as he can to gather in all he can get and hold tight; but it requires a great deal of exertion to open the arms and give out something.

*** ***

Other men judge us not so much by what we preach, as by the product˙of our preaching.

*** ***

The fundamental thing for a Latter-day Saint is to value his word as faithfully as his bond; to make up his mind that under no circumstances, no matter how hard it may be, by and with the help of the Lord, he will dedicate his life and his best energies to making good his promises.

*** ***

By the mere exertion of the will, by mere desire, we accomplish nothing; we must put with that desire the labor to accomplish the things we desire.

*** ***

When men stop praying for God's Spirit, they place confidence in their own unaided reason, and they gradually lose the Spirit of God.

*** ***

The chief secret of success is nothing more than doing what you can do well, without thought of fame. If fame comes at all, it will come because it is deserved, not because it is sought after.

When President Grant went to New York City, he had no difficulty whatever in finding his way about in the winding and confusing streets of lower Manhattan, where the great financial and industrial institutions of the nation have headquarters. The chief executives of these institutions, financial wizards, so to speak, were his personal friends. They welcomed him warmly when he entered their offices. Their doors were never closed to President Grant. They seemed always delighted to entertain him at lunch, to listen with rapt attention as he related the thrilling and unusual experiences of his life, of which he had had such an abundance.

Into these experiences, as he recited them, were frequently woven incidents of a faith-promoting nature, the struggles of the Saints, accomplishments of the Church, and the faith of the people. These hard-headed, practical businessmen, who in their daily lives and social contacts were accustomed to encounter deception, perversion of facts, and evasions of truth, found in President Grant a man of simple faith, one whose utter frankness bespoke an honesty that could be relied upon implicitly, a man who was willing to tell in detail the intimate facts of his life and not given to exaggeration. These friends greatly admired him for these traits of character.

Whether in the presence of the chairman of the board of a multibillion dollar banking institution, the president of a great railroad or insurance company, the head of a famed institution of learning, or in the home of the humblest wage earner or tiller of the soil, President Grant was at perfect ease and would generally lead out in the conversation.

To all who knew him, his life was an open book. His utter frankness was a distinguishing characteristic. He was honest in his faith and testimony. He never deceived anyone, nor had he any desire ever to do so. He was truly one of the greatest ambassadors of friendship and goodwill to the professional and business men that the Church has ever had. No one can begin to estimate the great good he did in the matter of allaying prejudice in the minds of influential people.

In the home of the humblest he was as welcome and content as in the mansion of the wealthy. Bread and milk and the simplest fare when offered him in the homes of the Saints were gratefully received and even more highly appreciated than the choicest foods that the famous chefs of the great hotels could prepare. The privilege of partaking of the hospitality of true Latter-day Saints, who always gave him the best that the land affords, always brought him joy and satisfaction. He never ceased to relate to them the goodness of the Lord to him, and he always appreciated being asked to join with them in prayer in the family circle.

He will always be remembered for his fervent, sincere,

and fearless testimony. No one in our time was blessed
with a stronger testimony of the truthfulness of the
restored gospel. Surely no one was more diligent in
bearing that testimony to the people of the world. He
never hesitated to let it be known that the truths of the
gospel and his love for them were the most important
treasures of his life. Those who heard him bear witness
to the goodness of the Lord could never honestly
question his sincerity.

In President Grant's mind no doubt ever existed
regarding the divinity of the work in which we are engaged; he knew that he was indeed God's chosen earthly
representative in the position he occupied. In childlike
faith he approached his Father in heaven, and his
prayers were often answered in miraculous ways. The
Lord talked to him through the revelations of his Spirit
and inspired him with the wisdom and guidance he
needed in his vast responsibilities. Both at home and
abroad, on land and on the sea, wherever his travels
took him, he bore fervent testimony to the divine truth.
Many thousands were stimulated to righteous living
and strengthened in their faith as they listened to his
clear and forceful voice fearlessly declaring:

I know, as I know that I live, that God lives; that Jesus is the
Christ; that Joseph Smith was a prophet of the true and living
God; that the Gospel commonly called Mormonism is in very deed
the Gospel of the Lord Jesus Christ, with every gift, grace, power
and blessing that was enjoyed in the former days.

President Grant's penchant for work developed the
latent powers within him. His faith in God and his
simplicity of character enabled him to obtain from divine
sources the inspiration to lead and direct his own course
of life in right channels. He was a true servant of God,
wholly worthy of the position he occupied. Certainly he
whom the Lord thus honored and so greatly magnified
earned the love, respect, and support of the Saints whose
welfare and blessing he so earnestly sought and devoutly
prayed for, and of sincere lovers of truth everywhere.

As I think back about President Grant and the near quarter of a century I was so closely associated with him, I am more than ever convinced that he was the man the Lord had prepared to lead his church and kingdom during those years. And what I say of President Grant I know of personal experience is true of the other leaders who have followed him in this great responsibility. Each one did not attain his position merely by accident or birth. That is not the Lord's way of selecting his prophets. In the preexistent world, when the Lord chose his leaders to send to the earth during the various dispensations of his providence, Heber J. Grant, George Albert Smith, David O. McKay, Joseph Fielding Smith, and Harold B. Lee had undoubtedly manifested those traits of character, abilities, and qualifications that befit them for the work to be entrusted to them in their generation of time. I am a firm believer in the truism that "the Lord has the right man in the right place at the right time to lead his earthly kingdom."

Having now given this word picture of President Grant, I feel it worthwhile to relate some of the many experiences of his life—many of them I enjoyed with him—that will show his greatness of character, his faith, integrity and devotion to the work of the Lord. This I feel especially privileged to do because I was so close to him, traveling with him constantly and enjoying his frankness and confidence for so many years.

President Grant was very considerate of nonmember visitors and guests who used tobacco. He always delighted to take his friends, especially those from the East, for rides into the beautiful canyons. He would arrange to stop along the way so that his guests could get out of the car, and he would conveniently disappear for a time so that the guests could have their smokes if they desired.

He particularly liked to take his friends and guests up American Fork Canyon and around the Mount

Timpanogos loop. He took this ride many, many times and always was delighted himself with the beautiful scenery and pleased when his friends also could enjoy these experiences, which were unusual for them. Frequently on these trips he would entertain his guests by singing in his strong voice "O Ye Mountains High" and other appropriate hymns.

One of the great virtues so manifested by President Grant was his honesty. In this he set a worthy, exemplary pattern. If he had a piece of property to sell and there was something about it of an undesirable nature he would not think of withholding that information from the prospective buyer. He was extremely honest in meeting his obligations. At times in his life he had been in financial difficulty, even near the point of bankruptcy, but he could never rest until all those obligations were liquidated.

President Heber J. Grant and his wife, Mrs. Augusta Winters Grant, at a community dinner honoring the president on his eightieth birthday.

While he was president it became necessary for him to undergo serious surgery. Because of the nature of the trouble and his being president of the Church, local doctors did not want to assume the responsibility for the operation but wanted the benefit of the best surgical skill available. Accordingly they recommended that he be sent to a specialist at the Presbyterian Hospital in Chicago. The operation was successful, and he was naturally very grateful to the surgeon for his skillful service.

When President Grant returned home, the doctor sent his bill and the amount was somewhat shocking—$2,500. He wrote the doctor and enclosed a statement of his financial condition, saying he thought the doctor considered him a wealthy man, being president of the Church and a director of a number of corporations. He said he felt that the doctor in reading his financial statement would understand that he was not wealthy, and if the doctor felt to discount his bill it would be greatly appreciated.

The doctor responded kindly and discounted the bill by $1,000 and President Grant gladly paid the $1,500. Some two or three years later when his financial condition had improved, he had pleasure in sending the doctor his check for the other $1,000.

Another experience of a somewhat similar nature emphasizing his honesty in all dealings occurred in connection with the Salt Lake Theater. He loved the theater. He had taken small parts on the stage when he was a child. He loved drama and good plays and frequented the Salt Lake Theater. He became a heavy stockholder in it. The time came when the theater was losing money and the stock decreased very seriously in market value. Knowing that two women, the daughters of an old friend of his in Grantsville, had some stock and could ill afford to lose the money they had invested, he purchased their stock at the price they paid for it, which was very much in excess of the market value.

As the years went by and it was decided to tear down the theater and sell the property, President Grant thought of the two widows in Grantsville whose stock he had purchased. The sale of the theater and the property on which it stood brought a sufficient sum that the stockholders received a substantial profit on their investment. President Grant sent his check to these good women to cover the amount that they would have received had they held on to their stock.

No one will ever know how many mortgages on homes of widows he paid out of his own funds. Time and again he would inquire as to his bank balance. He had no special interest in the accumulation of money except for the good he could do with it.

Perhaps not too many readers today are familiar with the gift of tongues and prophecy as they relate to President Grant's call to the apostleship and as president of the Church. On occasion he related the following interesting experiences:

My mother was the president of the Female Relief Society in the ward where I was born for over thirty years. She resigned only after she had lost her hearing. I grew up in the Relief Society meetings from the time I was a little boy.

*** ***

Upon one occasion Eliza R. Snow had the gift of tongues, and she gave a blessing to each and all of the sisters in a meeting of the presidents of different Ward Relief Societies, and my mother told me that each and every one of these blessings was fulfilled to the very letter, and the interpretation was given by Zina D. Young. Mother asked me when I became one of the Apostles if I remembered that meeting, while I was playing on the floor as a child. I told her yes, but I did not remember anything that was said, with the exception of just one sentence by Zina D. Young. Mother said, "Of course you could not understand Sister Snow, because she was speaking by the gift of tongues." I said, "I remember that Sister Zina raised her hand and said I would become a great big man." Mother said, "She didn't say anything of the kind; she said you would become a great man in the Church, and become an Apostle of the Lord Jesus Christ; it had no such meaning as that you should grow tall."

*** ***

I was in a ruined condition financially because of the panic of 1893. My wife who is dead promised me by the gift of tongues that I should live to pay all of my debts, and all of my friends thought I never could, but I did.

*** ***

My wife who is dead, when I was operated upon for appendicitis—the one who gave me this blessing by the gift of tongues—appeared to my wife who is living, and told her that no matter how sick I was, how near I came to death, I would not die, because my labor was not finished and that I should live to preach the Gospel in many lands and many climes. There were ten doctors present at my operation—nine said I must die because blood poisoning in the last stage had set in, but the promise was made by my wife who is in heaven that I should live, and I did live.

*** ***

As a young boy I had two very dear friends. We were called "the three inseparables." One of them was Feramorz L. Young and one was Richard W. Young. One was a son and the other a grandson of Brigham Young. My nearest friend was Fere. He went on a mission to Mexico. While coming home from his mission he died and was buried in the Gulf of Mexico. His companion, one of the apostles, made a report to his mother that he was one of the finest young men he had ever known in his life, and the mother answered that from a little child to the time of his death, he had never given her the slightest sorrow. She could not think of an act he had performed or a word he had uttered that she could not endorse. Perhaps some other mothers could say the same thing about their sons, but if the nearest and the most intimate boy friend could tell what he knew of the boy, perhaps the mother could not say that. As the nearest friend of Feramorz Young, I can say I never knew him to say a word or do a thing that was not absolutely right. If a man or a boy started to tell a story that could not be told to a lady, Fere Young would turn and walk away. He was the sweetest spirited boy I ever knew.

The following is taken from a letter written by President Grant regarding his call to the apostleship the spirit of revelation, and related matters:

My dear Brother:

President John Taylor, at the time that George Teasdale and I

were called to be Apostles and Seymour B. Young to be one of the
Seven Presidents of Seventy, gave to the Church a printed revelation which was voted upon and accepted by the Church. None of
the successors to President Taylor have published any revelations
similar to those that are contained in the Doctrine and Covenants.
The leaders of the Church who have succeeded President John
Taylor have been blessed with the spirit of revelation in guiding
the church.

Speaking of revelation by the spirit, you will find the following
in Section 8 of the Doctrine and Covenants, starting with the 2nd
verse:

> "Yea, behold, I will tell you in your mind and in your heart,
> by the Holy Ghost, which shall come upon you and which shall
> dwell in your heart.

> "Now, behold, this is the spirit of revelation; behold, this is
> the spirit by which Moses brought the children of Israel through
> the Red Sea on dry ground."

And again, in Section 9, starting with verse 7:

> "Behold, you have not understood; you have supposed that
> I would give it unto you, when you took no thought save it was
> to ask me.

> "But, behold, I say unto you, that you must study it out in
> in your mind; then you must ask me if it be right, and if it is
> right, I will cause that your bosom shall burn within you; there-
> fore you shall feel that it is right.

> "But if it be not right you shall have no such feelings, but
> you shall have a stupor of thought that shall cause you to forget
> the thing which is wrong; therefore, you cannot write that
> which is sacred save it be given you from me."

I had no thought whatever, at the time I was made the President
of the Church, of nominating Melvin J. Ballard to be an apostle;
my mind had rested upon another man for this position. But, I
supplicated the Lord for days for the inspiration of his Spirit, or
revelation if you like to call it that, that my mind might become
perfectly clear in naming a man to fill the vacancy caused by my
elevation to the presidency; and there was no doubt whatever in
my mind that Brother Melvin J. Ballard was the man that the Lord
desired for this position. I do not claim to have had a direct revelation to be given in so many words to the people, as Brother Taylor
had when Brother Teasdale and I were called to be apostles.

Referring to calls to the apostleship reminds me of the fact that
when Brother Francis M. Lyman was presiding over the Tooele
Stake of Zion, the patriarch of that stake gave him a blessing and

stated that he should be called to be one of the Twelve Apostles of
the Lord Jesus Christ in this last dispensation. This patriarch, the
late John Rowberry, gave me a blessing in which he stated that I
should be taken from that position and become a leader of great
magnitude among the people, and I now stand at the head of the
church as its president. I think it is perfectly proper to say that
Brother Rowberry was inspired and was told in his mind that in
his heart by the Holy Ghost what should befall Brother Lyman and
myself in our future lives, and that it would be perfectly proper to
quote from the revelation to Oliver Cowdery, namely: "This is the
spirit of revelation; behold, this is the spirit by which Moses brought
the children of Israel through the Red Sea on dry ground." And it
was that same spirit that inspired Brother Rowberry to make these
promises to Brother Lyman and myself, which have been fulfilled
to the very letter.

You can feel perfectly safe, that the presidency and apostles of
the Church are entitled to and will receive the whisperings of the
Spirit of the Lord to them by the Holy Ghost to guide and direct
the affairs of the Church in the way and manner that shall be pleasing
and acceptable to our Heavenly Father, and for the best good of
the saints.

With kind regards,

Sincerely your friend and brother,
(signed) Heber J. Grant

About Brother Ballard, President Grant said he was
never in his home. He had never met his mother or any
of his brothers and sisters at that time. He had met his
father because he was a bishop in Cache Valley, and he
had met Brother Ballard many times. He then said:

When I became the president of the Church, I had the right to
name a man to succeed me in the Twelve. I told the Lord that he
knew whom I wanted because I had nominated him three times,
but now that it is my duty to nominate a man I want the witness
of the spirit from You whom to nominate ———, and the impression to me was to nominate Melvin J. Ballard.

Many good and faithful Saints came to President
Grant from time to time asking that he administer to
their loved ones who were sick, thinking that his
blessing would have the effect of healing the sick person, while a blessing by some humble elder or even a
bishop or stake president would not have the same

influence with the Lord. Some went to these brethren in various positions and, not getting the desired results, came to him as a last resort.

It is natural for us to leave no stone unturned when the lives of those we love are in jeopardy. However, it is not intended that we shall go on living forever in mortality, nor is it intended that the sick shall always recover. In spite of our love for our dear ones and our faith and knowledge that the Lord can and does hear our prayers and recognize the administrations of the priesthood, we must reconcile our thinking to the truth that God's ways are not necessarily man's ways and that we want his will to prevail.

Illustrative of President Grant's thinking on this subject, I quote a letter that he addressed to a brother and sister who wrote to him regarding their sick daughter:

I have your letter of December 21, in which you tell me of the affliction which has come to your youngest daughter, following a severe case of scarlet fever. That disease is certainly a dreadful one; it so frequently leaves in its wake some permanent physical ailment.

Born and reared in the Church, as you have been, I am sure I need only say to you that I as president of the Church have no greater authority or power in the matter of healing than any other man bearing the Melchizedek Priesthood. I have often thought that this is one of the great blessings which the Lord intended to flow to his children by reason of our priesthood organization, which brings into every home of those who live faithfully the healing power with all its attendant blessings which belong to that priesthood. If, therefore, you hold the Melchizedek Priesthood, as I assume you do, and if you are living righteously, as I trust you are, you yourself have as much power and authority in this matter as anyone else. If you feel you need help in the administration I would urge you to get in touch with the president of the mission, or if you happen to know the elders who are living in that area get in touch with the elders directly, who can assist you in the ordinance of administration.

The Lord has told us, as recorded in the 42nd Section of the Doctrine and Covenants, verse 44, referring to the sick: "And the elders of the Church, two or more, shall be called, and shall pray for and lay their hands upon them in my name."

In order that the members of the priesthood should come to a fuller sense of their rights, prerogatives, and power, so that they themselves and the other members of the Church shall be able more fully to enjoy the blessings of the priesthood, the Church has found it necessary, as a policy, rather to discourage the thought that administration by one of the General Authorities has any greater efficacy than administration by any other person holding the Melchizedek Priesthood, because, as indicated above, the results from administration come by reason of faith, and not by reason of official position. The Church has on more than one occasion found it necessary to discourage so-called "healers"— good men whom the Lord had blessed with the power of healing— from going about over the Church administering to the sick. The reason for this is not that the man who has the gift of healing shall not exercise that gift, but it is that the rank and file of the priesthood must be brought to feel their own duty and responsibility and powers, and the necessity for living as the Lord would have them live, in order that they may exercise those powers. If these so-called "healers" should travel around about the Church there would soon grow up an attitude and a practice which would result in throwing off the restraining against sin which the priesthood must ordinarily feel in their daily lives, and the great mass of our Church members would cease to feel the need for right living.

There is an added reason, but by no means the most important one, that because of the demands which would be made upon me, and which I have neither the time nor the strength to meet, I have found it necessary to ask, where similar requests have been made, that the people suffering apply to their local priesthood for help.

I shall be very glad to place your daughter's name upon the temple prayer roll, and I myself do pray that she may be restored to complete health.

I am sure that you will understand the need which I have, both as a personal matter and as a matter of Church organization, for making the above explanation and decision.

With the kindest well wishes to you and yours, with a prayer that your daughter may regain her full health and strength, and wishing you the Compliments of the Season, I am,

> Faithfully yours,
> (signed) Heber J. Grant

President Grant, on various occasions, related a
dream experienced by Patriarch John Rowberry of
the Tooele Stake. He dreamed that he was on a great
vessel and every once in awhile somebody fell overboard. Brother Rowberry finally fell overboard himself, and when he finished struggling in the water, he
came out into a most beautiful country, the most beautiful he had ever seen. He met Orson Pratt, and he asked
Brother Pratt to show him the homes of the Prophet
Joseph Smith and the Patriarch Hyrum Smith.

It seems that Brother Pratt, who was a member of
the Council of the Twelve, happened to be in Tooele
at that particular time when Brother Rowberry had
this dream, visiting the various wards in the stake.
Brother Rowberry related this dream to Brother Pratt
and asked him if he could give him the interpretation,
praying to the Lord that Brother Pratt would not ask
him who the man was that he met in his dream. He
did not want to tell Brother Pratt that he, Brother
Pratt, would precede him in death. Brother Pratt said,
"I will pray about it and if I get the interpretation I will
give it to you."

Brother Pratt was in Tooele County for several
weeks, and when he was getting ready to leave to return
to Salt Lake City, he said, "Brother Rowberry, I
prayed about your dream, and I got the interpretation."
He said, "That vessel that you saw represented the
world. You said that the majority of the people that
fell overboard you did not know. If you will write down
a list of those you did know, in the order in which they
fell overboard, I promise you that they will die in that
exact order, and I promise you that you shall go to
heaven and you shall meet the identical man whom you
met in your dream and when you meet him tell him that
the dream was from the Lord and that the interpretation
was also from the Lord through Brother Orson Pratt."

President Grant said that sometime later when he

was out in Tooele serving as the president of the stake, word was received by telegram that Brother Orson Pratt was in a very serious condition of health and requesting that they hold a prayer meeting in Grantsville and also in Tooele for Brother Pratt's recovery. They did so, and as Brother Grant and some others were going into the upper room of the meetinghouse to have the prayer circle, Brother Rowberry said to Brother Grant, "Heber, do you remember my dream?" Brother Grant said that he did. Brother Rowberry then said, "Well, it is all right to pray for him, but it is Brother Pratt's turn next."

Brother Pratt did not recover, and the Lord gave a revelation to President John Taylor calling George Teasdale and Heber J. Grant to be apostles of the Lord Jesus Christ. President Grant filled the vacancy in the Twelve caused by the death of Orson Pratt.

Some years later President Grant, as an apostle, was out in Tooele attending a stake conference, and Brother Rowberry was a speaker at one of the meetings. He was in very good health though he was an old man at that time. President Grant said that he spoke with a great deal of power and expressed his love for the gospel. After the meeting, he said to President Grant, "Brother Grant, do you remember my dream?" President Grant said he did.

The patriarch then explained that the people had died in the order in which he had seen them fall off that vessel, and that they were now all gone and it was his turn next, and he said, "I am the happiest man in all Tooele County." He said he could not wait to meet Brother Pratt and to meet Brother Grant's father and other men and women he had loved with all his heart. He said, "By the way, I will tell your father, Brother Grant, that you are doing very well as a young apostle." President Grant said that the next time he went to

Tooele Brother Rowberry had passed on, and he visited his grave.

When President Grant's daughter Lucy was only six months old she was very sick. The Grants were living in Tooele at the time, he being the stake president. He went to Patriarch Rowberry and asked him to come and administer to her, and after they had administered to the child, Brother Rowberry turned and said, "Did you get the witness of the spirit that your baby should live?"

President Grant said, "No, I did not."

Brother Rowberry said, "I did, and I know she is going to live." He told President Grant to go to the desk and get a piece of paper, and that he would give her a patriarchal blessing. He did give her a blessing and made remarkable promises to her about her future life, all of which were fulfilled to the very letter.

Some months after this Brother Rowberry met President Grant and said, "I want you to come to my office [he was the probate judge there] as I have a blessing in my heart for you, of a patriarchal nature." President Grant said he gave him a most wonderful and marvelous blessing, all of which was fulfilled to the very letter. After giving the blessing, Brother Rowberry said, "Brother Grant, when I had my hands on your head I saw something that I dared not put in your blessing." President Grant said of himself that he had an impression then, as a young man just 24 years of age when Brother Rowberry made that remark, that he should live to preside over the Church. He said that he never spoke of it to anyone until he became the president of the Church, and that he tried to persuade himself at the time and through the ensuing years that it could not be, that he was mistaken in that impression.

The Lord gives to his servants various gifts. Some have one gift and some another. Brother Rowberry had the still small voice of revelation, which comes to many as vividly and strongly as though it were with a great sound.

I recall an experience with President Grant one Sunday morning. I was superintendent of the 33rd Ward Sunday School in Salt Lake City at the time. He telephoned my home asking that I come at once to his home. Word was sent to me at the ward, and I immediately drove to his home. He asked me to write some things that were on his mind, and he dictated to me a prophecy pertaining to a political situation, which prophecy was literally fulfilled within a very few weeks.

The following experience which was related by President Grant, is of an interesting nature.

I am a firm believer, beyond the shadow of a doubt, in the divinity of the work in which we as Latter-day Saints are engaged. There is no doubt in my mind as to the truth of it. There is no doubt that when the Lord speaks through his servants in bestowing blessings, those blessings will be fulfilled . . .

I call to mind that the Apostles upon one occasion had a man that they were trying for neglect of duty, and felt that he was unworthy to occupy the position that he did occupy, and he plead and pled for an extension of opportunity to work, and finally a motion was made that he be dropped from the position that he was occupying, and it was seconded, and one of the brethren of the Council of the Twelve made a talk and prophesied in the name of the Lord Jesus Christ and by the authority of the Holy Priesthood that he held, that we would never have to take action against this man, that unless he repented of the methods he had employed in his careless labors, that he himself would cut the cord that bound him to his associates in the Church. Finally, a motion was made that he be given another chance.

Years later the man became very careless and indifferent and the President of the Church instructed the Apostles who had tried this man to take action, that his carelessness was such we should not endure his occupying a position of trust, and that we should take action. I have never had my faith tried, I believe, in my life, as much as during about three or four hours when the Apostles were in a meeting and the expressed purpose of the meeting was to take action regarding this individual—to think of that marvelous prophecy that was delivered by one of the Apostles years before and which thrilled me from the crown of my head to the tips of my toes like an electric shock, and here we were about to take action against this man, instead of him cutting the cord that bound us together.

We had been discussing another matter, and finally President Lorenzo Snow, who was then the President of the Council of the Twelve Apostles, hit the table and said, "I won't hear one more word. We were sent here by the Prophet of the Lord to take action on a certain individual who has neglected his duty, and here we are talking and talking and talking about an insignificant matter, and I will not listen to another word. We will now take action in connection with the case that has brought us together." A knock came upon the door, the door was opened and a letter was handed in. It was the resignation of this man about whom the prophecy had been uttered to the effect that he himself would cut the cord that bound him to a chain with the Brethren. It made a marvelous and profound impression upon my mind that the Lord does not allow prophecies made, or blessings given under the inspiration of the Lord to fall by the wayside, and that men occupying positions of importance, if they do not do their duty, it is only a question of time when they will lose their standing.

One of the great things that has made a profound impression upon my mind from my earliest manhood is that I have never known a man or woman in this Church who was upright, faithful in keeping the commandments of the Lord that ever lost his standing in the Church; they grow all the time, and I have had my faith strengthened by seeing people that occupied important positions in the Church, even Apostles of the Church, who were not obedient, who did not fulfill the duties and the obligations devolving upon them—I have seen them drift in the wrong direction and finally lose their standing.

If I were to discover that as men and women grew in the light and knowledge and testimony of the Gospel and in doing their duty, eventually they dropped out, it would frighten me, but from childhood I have never been frightened.

Being somewhat of a financial genius and having made many friends among the businessmen and financiers in the eastern part of the United States, President Grant often related some unusual experiences that showed that on many financial missions for the Church he was blessed and inspired of the Lord.

One such experience occurred in 1891 on his first trip to New York. There was a panic in the country, and money was being lent at the rate of one-half of one percent a day on the stock exchange in New York. Banks were failing; businessmen were going broke by the hundreds. President Grant went east for the purpose of raising money.

Before he started on his trip, President Woodruff gave Brother Grant a blessing in which he said that he would be able to get all the money he was going for, and in addition would have the privilege of obtaining more if necessary. He returned home after raising $136,000 and with a promise by wire from Chicago that he could have an additional $48,000 if needed, but it was not needed.

President Grant said he went with perfect assurance that President Woodruff's promise would be fulfilled, and he was not discouraged even though he was laughed at by some of the bankers that he approached.

He first called on a bank in Omaha and requested $12,000, which request was declined. He asked for $24,000 in Chicago and then $48,000 in New York, which requests were declined. He afterwards got the $48,000, $25,000, and $15,000 in New York. He then sent a wire to the Chicago bankers for $12,000 more, and they answered, "Send the note."

President Grant explained that President Woodruff was not a businessman; he was a farmer and an orchardist. He was, however, the greatest converter of people to the Church that we have had. More than 2,000 people were baptized by him on his first mission to England. He was the power that made for the success of the sugar business.

President Grant said he shed the bitterest tears of his life when he thought of a certain bank failing of which President Woodruff was the president. He went to New York for the purpose of raising money to save it. He said that one morning while he was in New York he jumped out of bed just before eight o'clock and got down on his knees and said, "O Lord, I do not ask you to work two miracles. Money is lending at one-half of one percent a day, or 182½ percent a year. O Lord, I do not ask you to send me a philanthropist to give me the money, but inspire some man to lend me $200,000 and charge me $50,000 for the privilege."

He then took a bath, took things very easy, ate his breakfast slowly, got on the elevated train, purchased a morning paper, and started to read it. Just before he reached the office of H.G. Claflin & Co., he thought to himself, "I will get off here and shake hands with John Claflin." He went into the office and was told that just about an hour earlier Mr. Claflin had left the office and said, "If you can possibly find Heber J. Grant, I want to see him."

President Grant said to himself, "He is the man who is going to lend me the money." He then asked the people in the office where he could find Mr. Claflin, and they answered they did not know, but they were to let him know where he could find Mr. Grant. President Grant told them that he would be at the National Park Bank as soon as he could get there, and that he would remain there until he heard from Mr. Claflin.

He got back on the elevated and commenced reading the paper again, and he went past the station where he should have gotten off for the National Park Bank. He felt very much annoyed because the next station was quite a distance away, and he would have to walk back or catch the streetcar to go to the National Park Bank. Greatly disappointed, he got off on Broad Street, which is one street east of Broadway, and was walking up the street to catch a streetcar when he saw a sign in a window, "Blake Brothers, Stock Brokers." He walked into the office and there he found Mr. Claflin and Charlie Blake talking together.

In the course of the conversation that ensued, Mr. Claflin said, "Grant, you once pounded the table and said a man was a fool who, if he had a couple of banks that were liable to go broke, and if he could get three or four hundred thousand dollars to save them, would hesitate a moment in paying $100,000 premium for the money. Charlie and I have been talking it over and Charlie has agreed to cash the notes of H.G. Claflin and Co. for $400,000 and we are going to divide the $100,000 you offered to give."

President Grant said, "Oh, I was just talking through my hat."

Mr. Claflin said: "Well, Mr. Grant, you know and I know that your bank and every other bank in the United States today is tottering, and you do not know how soon they are going to fail. You dare not look me in the eye and tell me that your bank is not in a dangerous condition."

President Grant answered, "Mr. Claflin, I do not want $400,000. I am sure that $200,000 would save my two banks, and I will gladly give you $50,000 provided you lend me $200,000 and will hand me a check right now for $50,000 to telegraph home this afternoon before the banks close." Mr. Claflin pulled his checkbook out of his pocket, wrote the check, and handed it to him, and Brother Grant telegraphed the money home. The balance came later.

He got 7½ percent instead of 6 percent because of the bonus of $50,000. He carried that note for three years. Brother Grant came home and arranged with the principal creditors to take care of them, told them the circumstances, and asked them to pay 12 percent for the money for three years. This saved both the banks, and the amount the banks had to pay on the bonus was $9,000 each. The 12 percent, which they were mighty glad to give, and only having to pay 7½ percent, made the loss to the banks only $9,000 each.

Mr. Claflin was one of the President's dearest friends from that time on.

President Grant seemed to have almost what some people would consider a mania regarding the sugar business. He felt the Lord had a purpose in establishing that institution, so that the farmers might have a cash crop to assist them in their economic conditions. The following excerpt from remarks of President Grant in Boulder City, Nevada, March 25, 1934, about the sugar industry and other matters, is indicative of his interest in this subject:

The Utah-Idaho Sugar Company had borrowed over ten million dollars. They had contracted for beets at $12 a ton when sugar was selling for $17 a bag, but when they had on hand 2,300,000 bags of sugar, the price of sugar had gone down to $5 a bag, and there was no sale for it, and we had the experience of losing $5,000,000 that year. We had borrowed over $10,000,000 and we needed more money for the next year's crop. We had only paid back $3,000,000, and the other $7,000,000 was past due, and we needed another $2,800,000 for our next crop. We did not need very much under the circumstances because the farmers were so mad because we had to reduce the payment to them. They did not stop to figure that we had given them $5,000,000 more than their beets were worth the year before.

Mr. Fred W. Shibley, an official of the Bankers Trust Company in New York, was sent out here representing the bankers of New York, San Francisco, and Chicago, to look into our affairs and to make a recommendation as to whether we should be declared bankrupt and turned over to the bankers to wind up our business, or what should be done. I am very grateful that he became thoroughly convinced that our business would eventually be successful. He went back into our books for between 20 and 25 years, and compiled a looseleaf book with various statistics consisting of nearly 200 pages, which he jokingly called "Book of Mormon," and he recommended to the bankers in New York that they renew our notes and give us the $2,800,000 additional on certain conditions and the condition was that $2,800,000 more be put into the Company as capital stock.

However, the bankers did not pay any attention to his optimistic report, and they declined to loan us the $2,800,000 necessary unless security was put up, and we had quite a time, but we finally did get a renewal, and we finally arranged with Uncle Sam to lend our Company the other $10,000.00 so we did not need any of the bankers' money. Then they finally concluded to lend us the money which they had refused to lend on the very security they had refused to accept. . . .

This man, Shibley, told me he was not a money-lender in his work as a banker, but he said, "I am a financial doctor, diagnosing the cases of sick financial institutions, and prescribing the remedy to cure them!" . . .

When I parted from him in Chicago he went on a fast train to New York, and I on a slow one. . . .

I said to him, "Mr. Shibley, I have thoroughly enjoyed my visit with you, and am grateful for this wonderful and optimistic report you are making of our company. . . . I would like you to promise me that between here and New York you will read two pamphlets that I want to give you. You are the vice-president of a great bank with hundreds of millions of dollars in assets, one of the greatest in all New York. You would not think of such a thing as reading these pamphlets when you get home, but promise me you will read them between here and New York." I handed him the pamphlet, "Joseph Smith Tells His Own Story," and also, "My Reasons for Leaving the Church of England and Joining the Church of Jesus Christ of Latter-day Saints," by Col. R. M. Bryce Thomas.

When I got to New York I called on him, and he said, "My life has been spent in analyzing things. As I have already told you, Mr. Grant, my business is to analyze the affairs of sick financial corporations. By every rule of my life to arrive at the truth, I have to acknowledge this story of Joseph Smith as true." I was told he had charge of looking into the affairs of the great General Motors Corporation at the time they were in distress when there was some fear of their failing many years ago, and was subsequently invited, after he made his report to the company, to become one of their directors. He made the statement: "No liar ever did write or could write such a story as the story told by Joseph Smith," and he was so excited when he said this that he pounded on the table and said, "A liar would never think, in describing an angel, to say his feet did not quite touch the floor. It would not enter his head. Nor to say that he had on a loose robe and that he could see into his breast. No liar ever deals in details, and this story deals in nothing but details—the hour, the place, the circumstances, the spot, the people—everything. Liars would not dare tell a story like that. They could not do it."

He said, "Of course, you know it is generally conceded that liars ought to have good memories and they are always deficient in that particular. Liars in business never give you a detailed statement. They just give you a lot of high points. If they gave you the

details of a business in a bad company, they would have no chance
of getting a continuation of notes, etc."

When he told me that, I thought, "I know now why you went
back for 20 long years on our books. You were looking for something crooked and could not find it."

He continued: "This man had the visions he claims to have had.
I do not expect to join your Church, but that story, by every rule
of my life, is the truth. Mr. Grant, I am a student. I am agnostic.
I do not accept it as the word of God. I only say to you that if I
actually believed the Bible to be the word of God, I would not be
an honest man after reading this pamphlet if I did not join your
Church. I say that no honest man who believes in the Bible can
get away from the proofs this man has given, with scriptural
references, to sustain your doctrine. They are unanswerable, I
maintain."

I had the privilege of meeting with President Grant
and Mr. Shibley in New York on two or three occasions.
Mr. Shibley impressed me as a man of great ability and
wisdom.

The experience of a visit to the King of Sweden was
related by President Grant on the occasion of the visit
of the Crown Princess and Prince of Denmark in the
Salt Lake Tabernacle on April 16, 1939.

On behalf of the Presidency of the Church we are very glad
indeed to have this very fine auditorium to tender to the committee that is welcoming our distinguished visitors. I say to our
distinguished visitors here that we have a very warm place in our
hearts not only for their country, but for the other Scandinavian
countries, and I might add Holland also, seeing that my mother
is Pennsylvania Dutch. . . .

It fell to my lot on the Fourth of July to be in Stockholm, and
I said to my wife and daughters, the President of the Swiss-German
Mission, the editor of our Star and our fine singers, Arvilla Clark
and Spencer Clawson, "What would you like to do to celebrate
our natal day?" I said, "I would like to call on King Oscar." They
said, "So would we." I said, "Go in and put on your best clothes
and I will write His Royal Highness a letter and take you over," (I
understood that he was on a little island and it would take about
a half hour to get there), "and I will introduce you to the king."

I wrote a letter to the King telling him I was from Utah and
that I hoped he would waive formalities, that I had letters of
introduction from senators asking that I be given an audience and

that I had not time to have those letters presented in regular form, and this being the day of all days to Americans I hoped he would waive formality and give us an audience.

We went to the little island and there was a soldier with a gun over his shoulder walking back and forth. I said to our party, "We will wait until he gets right close to us and then turns around and by the time he gets to the other end of his walk and turns around I will have made arrangements for the interview. I am not afraid at all that he will shoot me, because he will feel sure that I would not dare be there if I hadn't authority to be there." I told them that when I had arranged the interview I would motion for them to come in.

I knocked at the door and a man came who undoubtedly talked Swedish. I did not understand him. I talked English. He shut the door and turned the key. I feel sure he thought there was some crazy man outside. Pretty soon a gentleman came who talked perfect English, and he said, "What can I do for you?"

I said, "I desire to see King Oscar."

He said, "You cannot see King Oscar. No one can see the King unless properly presented."

I said, "Did the King tell you he would not see me?"

He said, "No."

"I do not take any answer from you, sir, I sent a letter of introduction to the king from the Governor of the great State of Utah." I told Governor Heber M. Wells who wrote the letter to make it as strong as his conscience would let him, and to be sure that his signature was attested by the Secretary of State, and also to be sure to put the seal of the State on it with a long red ribbon attached. I told him I was sure that would get me an introduction anywhere I went. I decided that I would be willing to lose that letter if I could get to see King Oscar. I had sent the letter in and told him I hoped this letter would answer the purpose, waiving formalities. When this man refused me admittance I said: "You bring my letter back; I am not going to take any message from you. The letter I sent in to the king was from the Governor of the *great state of Utah*"—and I emphasized the *GREAT STATE OF UTAH*.

He came back and said: "The king will receive your party. Invite them to come, and he will receive you here on the lawn." I motioned to them and they came.

After we had asked two or three questions back and forth, the king said, "Mr. Grant, how many of your people here (there were about sixteen of us) speak Swedish?" There were only three, so he changed to perfect English. He was a magnificent specimen

of humanity; he stood over 6 ft. high, as straight as an arrow. He
was very, very courteous indeed. He asked many questions about
our people, what they were doing there, etc. And then he said, "I
want to tell you something, Mr. Grant. I have sent my representatives to different parts of the United States of America, to inquire
how the former citizens of my country were getting along in Wis-
consin and in other parts of the United States, and I want you to
know, Mr. Grant, that in no other part of the United States of
America are the former citizens of my country as prosperous,
as happy, and as contented as in Utah. All the various churches
here have petitioned me time and again to have you Mormons
refused the privilege of preaching in this country, but having received this report, I want you to know that as long as I am the
King of Sweden and Norway, perfect and absolute liberty shall
be granted to you Mormons."

I felt pleased about that, and I consider King Oscar one of the
great kings in Europe.

I met many great and notable people with President
Grant. This was a rare privilege.

I enjoyed very much the privilege of meeting Edgar
A. Guest, the poet, when President Grant and I called
on him at his home in the outskirts of Detroit, Michigan. Mr. Guest had a very comfortable and attractive
home, and we spent some little time visiting with him
and his young daughter. He was a very genial host, and
we thoroughly enjoyed spending an hour or two with
him in his home.

Mr. Guest appeared to have a high regard for
President Grant, and I feel sure that he did have, although much of that regard may have stemmed from the
fact that President Grant purchased and distributed
thousands of copies of Mr. Guest's books *A Heap O'
Livin', The Path to Home,* etc. In addition to being a
writer of popular verse, he was in constant demand as
a lecturer.

Some people claim that Mr. Guest was not a true
poet, just a rhymer, but I must admit that his sentiments reach the heart and impress the hearer or the
reader with a better understanding of the important

things in life. His poem entitled "True Nobility" is one of the many poems that President Grant loved.

Carl R. Gray, who for some years was president of the Union Pacific Railroad, was a gentleman in every sense of the term, and it was a pleasure to visit with him on various occasions with President Grant. His home was in Omaha, Nebraska, but the head offices of the railroad were in New York. Mr. Gray's wife was a very fine woman of high principle and of great faith. She was not a member of The Church of Jesus Christ of Latter-day Saints, but she was a prominent speaker on religious subjects. I have met few, if any, men, non-members of the Church in high political or industrial positions, who impressed me more favorably as a man of character and integrity than Carl R. Gray. Needless to say, Mr. Gray held President Grant in high esteem and the president had a real affection for him.

An interesting person on whom President Grant frequently called was Charles G. Dawes, a former vice-president of the United States. Mr. Dawes was president of the First National Bank of Chicago, and President Grant frequently called on him at his office in the bank. Mr. Dawes had the highest regard for Reed Smoot, an apostle of the Church and U.S. Senator from Utah, and also for Wilson McCarthy, also a member of the Church with whom Mr. Dawes had been closely associated while in Washington.

I was very much intrigued by one of Mr. Dawes' mannerisms. He loved to smoke a pipe, and we never called on him that he did not take his pipe in his hand, open one of the drawers in his desk, take out a tin of pipe tobacco, load the bowl of his pipe, and strike a match as if to light the pipe. But never did I see him light the pipe or smoke it. He would hold the tobacco-filled pipe in one hand and the lighted match in the other as he conversed with the president. The match would go out, and he would light another, but always

with the same result. I presume he failed to light the
pipe and smoke it out of deference to President Grant,
but each time we called he went through the same cere-
mony.

It was my pleasure on one occasion with President
Grant to call on George Sutherland, who at that time
was one of the Justices of the Supreme Court of the
United States. Our visit was in one of the prominent
dinner clubs in Washington. The following story was
related by President Grant, but Judge Sutherland repeated it on this occasion more or less the way it is
set down here.

Justice Sutherland told of how upon one occasion
when the boys at the Brigham Young University were
ridiculing him because he did not study the Book of
Mormon, he got mad and used language that was such
as could have caused him to be expelled from school.
He expected the next day to be expelled. Brother Maeser
got up in the assembly the following day and instead
of expelling him quoted the Article of Faith that we
allow all men the privilege of worshiping how, where, or
what they may, and chastised the boys who had been
abusing a student who had been invited to come to the
school and who had asked for the privilege of coming
and had said he wanted to be excused from studying
the Book of Mormon and other religious subjects. He
said that you do not believe in your own faith when
you ridicule a man for not studying what he does not
want to study.

Justice Sutherland said, "Immediately after the
morning devotional service was over I rushed up to
Brother Maeser's desk and said, 'Dr. Maeser, I take
Book of Mormon from this day, and I will pass as good
an examination, if not better, than any of the other
boys'." And he did.

Sutherland never became a member of the Church,
but he was always a staunch supporter, and on the oc-

casion referred to when President Grant and I visited with him he remarked that he believed that he had done and was doing more for the Church than if he were a member. There was no question that his heart was with the Church and that he was indeed converted to its truths.

A very interesting friend and acquaintance was Dr. Henry C. Link, author of *The Return to Religion* and other books. Dr. Link seemed to have a very high regard for President Grant, and I had the privilege of being with them on several occasions when President Grant called on him at his office. He was a man of high principles, and while he never joined the Church—he passed away a few years ago—the truths of the gospel seemed to find a responsive cord in his life.

An interesting story by President Grant relates to Karl G. Maeser.

Brother Franklin D. Richards came over to Germany from England to be present at the baptism of the first convert in Saxony where Brother Karl G. Maeser resided. Brother Richards presided over the European Mission, and he felt he would like to be present at the gathering of the first fruits of the gospel in that land.

Brother Willam Budge, subsequently the president of the Bear Lake Stake of Zion, and who finally ended his life as the president of the Logan Temple, was then in charge of our missionary work in Switzerland where there was liberty, and missionaries were sent occasionally into the German empire.

They went out at midnight to perform the baptism and while coming back from the place where Brother Maeser was baptized, together with his wife, brother-in-law, and other members of the family, Brother Maeser was conversing with President Franklin D. Richards. After a few questions had been asked and interpreted by Brother Budge, Brother Maeser asked Brother Budge not to interpret the answers, that he understood them perfectly. And then Brother Franklin D. Richards said, "Do not interpret the questions. I understand them." They walked for miles, Karl G. Maeser asking questions in German, Franklin D. Richards answering them in English, neither understanding the other's language, and yet, under the inspiration of the Lord, both understanding each other perfectly. They finally came to the River Elbe. There was a bridge

there that they had to go over to get into the city of Dresden. . . .
when they got on the opposite side of the bridge—they had been
separated as they crossed the bridge—when they came together
again, Brother Maeser asked a question and Brother Richards
turned to Brother Budge and said, "Brother Budge, I do not understand a word of that question. Please interpret it." And then
Brother Maeser said, "Brother Budge, interpret the answer, I do
not understand a word of it," and he did so.

The next question was, "Apostle Richards, why have we been
able to understand each other for miles, and now all of a sudden we
cannot understand a word?" And the answer was, "Brother Maeser,
one of the fruits of the gospel of the Lord Jesus Christ, the true
gospel of Christ, is the interpretation of tongues. The Lord has
permitted you to partake of one of the fruits of the gospel. No
tree without leaves and without fruit is of any value, but a tree
that has the leaves and the fruit growing upon it—if you and I can
walk up to that tree and reach out our hands and pluck the fruit
and partake of it, nobody on earth could convince us that the
tree was not alive." Brother Maeser in this particular case had had
the privilege of reaching out his hand and plucking one of the
fruits that grow upon the gospel tree, namely, the interpretation of
tongues, which had also been given to Brother Franklin D.
Richards.

Brother Richards said to him: "Brother Maeser, the Lord has
given to you a new witness and testimony that you have found the
truth; he has allowed you and me this night to have a complete
interpretation of tongues; God has given to you, Brother Maeser,
a witness that you have really found the gospel of his Son, Jesus
Christ."

Brother Maeser told me that he trembled like a leaf, and that
he looked up into heaven and he said to the Lord: "Father, thou
hast heard and answered my prayer, and I once more dedicate to
thee, if need be, my life for this gospel."

As President Grant said, those who knew Brother
Maeser know that he gave his life to the Church. "No
man within my acquaintance was ever more faithful,
more diligent, more unselfish in his labors and more
consistent and peristent in working for the salvation of
the youth of Zion than was Karl G. Maeser."

It was my good fortune while in Germany with
President Grant in 1947 to visit the old home of Brother
Maeser in Meissen. As I recall the experiences now,
a woman perhaps in her sixties was living there and was

kind enough to show us through the home, which was a very fine little place and was in first-class condition at the time.

I think one of the most unique, and yet one of the most inspirational, experiences I had with President Grant occurred Sunday, September 5, 1937, as we were returning home from Europe, the president having completed a tour of the missions in Europe. We shared the same cabin on the ship. It was the S.S. Empress of Australia. It being the first Sunday of the month, and a fast day, he decided that he and I would hold a testimony meeting of our own. At the time he lacked only two months of being 81.

Accordingly, the two of us sang the hymn "God Moves in a Mysterious Way, His Wonders to Perform," after which I offered prayer and he bore his testimony. I wrote the testimony in shorthand as he gave it, and the following are excerpts therefrom:

I feel that I would like to read what I have already marked in the first essay in the book, *The Power of Truth,* by William George Jordan.

The following particularly finds a wonderful response in my heart:

"Truth is the rock foundation of every great character. It is loyalty to the right as we see it; it is courageous living of our lives in harmony with our ideals; it is always—power.

"Truth ever defies full definition. Like electricity it can only be explained by noting its manifestation. It is the compass of the soul, the guardian of conscience, the final touchstone of right. Truth is the revelation of the ideal; but it is also an inspiration to realize that ideal, a constant impulse to live it. . . ."

How I do thank the Lord for the restoration of the true gospel of Jesus Christ. No words of mine can express my gratitude for an absolute knowledge of the divinity of the restored gospel through the instrumentality of Joseph Smith the Prophet.

I was very happy to make the acquaintance of Mr. Jordan, and spent many hours in his home in New York conversing with him. I wrote him a letter in 1909, and received the following reply:

172 W. Clark Street
New York
November 9, 1909

Dear Mr. Grant:

I thank you for the Book of Mormon, the tracts and the booklet on 'Utah' which have just come to hand, and for the special number of the Era which will probably come by a later post. I shall read them with pleasure and interest. From what I know of your church, I believe it is doing live, practical work for the betterment of humanity and that, more than any other church's, your creed is transferred into living; it is not a theory of life service but a simple faith manifested in works.

No religion is worth anything unless it yields dividends— dividends of finer individual lives of truer brotherhood, of higher uplift in the affairs of everyday life. I trust some time it may be my privilege, and it would surely be my pleasure, to visit your people and view the work at close range. I wish there were more tolerance between the sects and denominations, and that the world's walls of tolerance and ignorant criticism were torn down. It is not necessary that we should accept each other's faith in order to respect it and to have reverence for that which is inspiring men to finer living.

Believe me,

Very gratefully and sincerely yours,
(signed) William George Jordan

Mr. Jordan is the author of very many books, every one of which that I have read has made a very profound impression upon me.

I can truthfully say this morning that never in my life have I had a greater desire to grow in the light and knowledge of the gospel, in capacity to live it, and in capacity to inspire others to live it, and in capacity to accomplish more for the redemption of the wayward and to bless those that are in distress in the Church, than I do this day. And I thank God from the bottom of my heart on this fast day for an absolute testimony of the divinity of the work in which I am engaged, and for a knowledge that God lives, that Jesus is the Christ, the Son of the living God, the Redeemer of the world, and that Joseph Smith is a prophet. . . .

I have read in the scripture that when two or three assemble in the name of the Lord, "there will I be also." I believe that the Lord has been with us here today, although there are only two of us.

President Grant offered the following prayer at the close of the meeting:

O God, our Heavenly and Eternal Father, we thy servants, in dismissing this little meeting, approach thee in gratitude for our knowledge of the divinity of the work in which we are engaged, and pray that our minds may never become darkened, and that we may grow in the light and knowledge and testimony of the gospel to the end of our lives, and this we ask in all humility in the name of thy Son, Jesus Christ. Amen.

Others, too, had special feelings toward President Grant with perhaps a greater skill at expressing them, but with no greater sincerity and appreciation. I quote two of these which I have kept in my scrapbook as special tributes to a great man.

The following is from President J. Reuben Clark, a counselor and faithful, loyal friend to President Grant:

God fashioned him in heart and mind and body, in ability, in experience, and in wisdom, just as he has fashioned every man whom he has ever called to lead his people, even from Moses of old till now. No man ever comes to lead God's people whom he has not trained for the task. . . .

He so lived his life that it had no dark places across which he must draw a curtain. His life had nothing to embarrass, nothing to hide, nothing of which he must be ashamed.

He was completely fearless. Sin and corruption could not be so highly placed as not to meet his rebuke.

Truth was the sole guide of his life; error never led him down the wrong track.

He had the pure and undefiled religion of James: he visited the fatherless and the widows in their affliction and kept himself unspotted from the world.

Another was from Noble Warrum, who wrote the following editorial in the *Salt Lake Tribune:*

Tall, slender, bearded, gray and grave, of striking appearance and patriarchal bearing, President Grant might have stepped forward from an illustrated page of the Old Testament. Had he lived in those far distant days he would have seemed, and no doubt felt, at ease and at home in the tents of Abraham, Isaac and Jacob.

He would have taken high rank among the potentates and prophets of olden times as a shrewd and sagacious director of temporal affairs, a rigid disciplinarian in spiritual matters, a methodical chronicler of passing events, an indulgent but observant father to his people, and a valiant crusader against the mockers of Jehovah and his commandments.

Modern minded, well groomed, and up-to-date, he will be remembered, yet it would have required no great stretch of the imagination to picture him leading the Children of Israel through the wilderness, counseling with the tribesmen of Canaan about their flocks and herds, hurling anathemas at idolators from the foot of Sinai, driving the chariot of Jehu toward Jezreel, swinging the sword of Gideon against the Midianites, smiting the walls of Jericho in righteous wrath, or marching at the head of a triumphant legion singing hosannas to the Highest.

Now I find this closing thought appropriate at this time. I had an interesting visit with President Heber J. Grant a day or two before he passed away. Among other things, he said, "Joseph, have I ever been unkind to you?" And I was happy to be able to say, "You never have been." I realize that as time passes we are inclined to forget the unpleasant things and remember only that which is pleasing, but I am sincere in saying that President Grant never said an unkind word to me during the 23 years I worked with him. No two men could have been closer to each other than we were. There was nothing in his life that he withheld from me, and I knew the innermost desires of his heart. He was a great and noble spirit, truly one of God's chosen noblemen.

3

Counselors to President Grant

President Heber J. Grant had an array of extremely strong and competent counselors during the nearly 27 years he was president of the Church. His length of service was exceeded only by that of President Brigham Young, who served 30 years as Church president.

When President Grant became president on November 23, 1918, he retained the same two counselors as his predecessor, President Joseph F. Smith. These counselors were Anthon H. Lund, first counselor, and Charles W. Penrose, second counselor. Since President Lund died in March 1921 and I did not go into the First Presidency's office until 1922, I did not become acquainted with him in his office as first counselor, though I was aware of his great leadership and service to the Church and had heard him speak on numerous occasions.

As I have previously mentioned, the First Presidency at the time my service in the office began consisted of President Grant, President Penrose as first counselor, and President Anthony W. Ivins as second counselor. Thus the counselors to President Grant during my long and intimate association as

When the author began his service with President Grant, the counselors were Charles W. Penrose and Anthony W. Ivins. Charles W. Nibley came into the First Presidency at the death of President Penrose in 1925.

his secretary and as secretary to the First Presidency
were as follows:

Charles W. Penrose—first counselor, March 1921 to
May 1925

Anthony W. Ivins—second counselor, March 1921
to May 1925—first counselor, May 1925 to
September 1934

Charles W. Nibley—second counselor, May 1925 to
December 1931

J. Reuben Clark, Jr.—second counselor, April 1933
to October 1934—first counselor, October 1934
to May 1945

David O. McKay—second counselor, October 1934
to May 1945

As can be seen, I served longer with President
Clark and President McKay than with the other
counselors, since they also were counselors to President George Albert Smith. It is my desire in this
chapter to help my readers to become briefly acquainted with the above named counselors. However,
I have taken the liberty to go much more extensively
into my association with President Clark than with
the others, and I feel justified in doing so because of
the closeness I felt to that great man. I have often
said that the two most influential men in my life,
who were to me as a father would be, were President
Grant and President Clark. President McKay will be
more extensively introduced in the chapter of this
book which deals with his nearly 20 years of service
as president of the Church and my work and close
association with him during the time he was a
counselor to two presidents and then president of
the Church—a total of about 36 years.

PRESIDENT CHARLES W. PENROSE

Even though he was advanced in age—he was past his ninetieth birthday when I started to work in the office of the First Presidency—I quickly found President Charles W. Penrose, an alert and capable man, had well earned the reputation applied by his friends as "one of the ablest and best informed men among the leaders of the Church."

He had a rapid style of preaching, and his use of plain language in effective expression made a lasting impression on all who heard him. Essentially a journalist and missionary, the English convert rose to great heights of church leadership, as a preacher of the gospel and defender of the faith through the spoken word and the might of his pen. Though called to the apostleship in 1904 at the age of 72, he became at once a pillar of strength to the Church and the brethren with whom he associated.

At the time he was chosen an apostle, President Penrose was already well known throughout the Church, perhaps more through his extensive writings than any other way. When called to the Twelve, he was serving as editor-in-chief of the *Deseret News,* the Church's official newspaper, published in Salt Lake City. He had held that position since President Lorenzo Snow called him home in 1899 from England, where he had been serving his third mission in his native land. Not only was he a dedicated journalist and missionary, but also as a preacher, writer, and debater he had few equals.

Perhaps one can better understand the achievements of this dedicated Mormon leader when he knows something of his earliest years. He was born on February 4, 1832, at Camberwell, London, England. In very early life he was known by his family and associates as a boy of studious and in-

quiring mind, quick in perception and having a remarkable memory. He read the scriptures when he
was only four years old and thus laid an early
foundation for what was to be a remarkable career
as a missionary and religious leader.

He was attracted to the teachings of the first
Latter-day Saint missionaries he heard in London—
especially to the logic of their reasoning and their
teaching from the scriptures with which he was so
familiar. At the age of 18 he joined the Church,
the only member of his family to do so. He left
almost immediately on a mission, actually without
purse or scrip, having only the clothes he wore.
He walked the distance from London to Maldon in
Essex County with bleeding feet and began a labor
of love that lasted for seven years. He met with
unusual success, enjoyed frequently the gift of healing, and left an indelible mark on the missionary
history of Great Britain to which he was to add
considerably in the years to come.

He was then called to preside over the London
Conference (district). During these years his pen was
also very busy. His thorough understanding of the
gospel and his skill at writing were combined to
produce numerous articles for the *Millennial Star,*
Church organ published in Britain for the European
missions. One of his biographers wrote: "Out of
the silken and golden threads of his poetical
thoughts and emotions, [he] wove the fabric of
those beautiful thoughts of Zion which have cheered
the hearts and fired with patriotism and holy zeal
the drooping souls of thousands."

After a total of ten years as missionary and
writer in the ministry in his own land, he was released in 1861 and came to Zion. He drove his ox
team across the plains with his family, being 11
weeks on the trip. Imagine the rejoicing in his soul

when he at last reached the Zion of his dreams, the
Zion of which he had written beautiful poetry put
to song several years before he saw it in person!

Few Latter-day Saint hymns are sung today with
more fervor, appreciation, and frequency than his
"O Ye Mountains High." I reprint here the first
stanza only to show the longing of President Penrose
for Zion and the miracle of his "vision" of the place,
since he wrote this song in 1854, while on his
mission in Essex, five years before coming to America:

> O ye mountains high, where the clear blue sky
> Arches over the vales of the free,
> Where the pure breezes blow and the clear streamlets flow,
> How I've longed to your bosom to flee!
> O Zion! dear Zion! land of the free,
> Now my own mountain home, unto thee I have come—
> All my fond hopes are centered in thee.

This song, as were all others by Charles W. Penrose,
was a favorite of President Heber J. Grant. On the
occasion of his sixtieth birthday, President Grant
and his wife hosted all the General Authorities of the
Church and their wives in a cottage in Brighton at the
head of Big Cottonwood Canyon, a few miles east of
Salt Lake City. Songs composed by President Penrose
were sung on that occasion, and he responded readily
when asked to explain the circumstances of the origin
of his hymns. Of the writing of "O Ye Mountains High"
he said that evening:

"O Ye Mountains High" was written somewhere along about
1854, published in 1856. I was walking on a dusty road in Essex.
My toes were blistered and my heels too. I had been promised
that if I would stay in the mission another year I should be released. That was the cry every year: "Brother Penrose, if you will
stay and labor another year, we will see that you are released to
go to Zion." But it kept up for over ten years. Of course I had read
about Zion, and heard about the streets of Salt Lake City, with
the clear streams of water on each side of the street, with shade
trees, and so on. I could see it in my mind's eye, and so I composed

that song as I was walking along the road, and set it to a tune—
the Scotch ditty, "Oh Minnie, Oh Minnie, Come O'er the Lea."
Those were the opening words. —When I got to the place called
Mundon, in Essex, we held a cottage meeting, and in that meeting I sang it for the first time it was ever sung. Of course the words
were adapted to a person who had never been to Zion then, but it
was afterwards changed in a very slight respect or two, to fit
people who had gathered with the Saints. It was inspirational
and seemed to please President Brigham Young. (George D.
Pyper, *Stories of Latter-day Saint Hymns, p.15.*)

From the day it was first published in 1856,
while its author was still a missionary in England,
the song, often referred to as "Zion," was instantly
one of the favored hymns of the Church.

Other songs in our present-day hymnbook by
President Penrose include "Beautiful Zion for Me,"
"God of Our Fathers, We Come unto Thee," "Up
Awake, Ye Defenders," and "School Thy Feelings,
O My Brother." There were many other poems and
songs written by this author, whose love of the gospel
was often expressed in poetic language.

Because it tells within itself the inner struggle
of this kindly but fearless defender of the faith and
tireless missionary, it would be well to tell the story
behind the writing of "School Thy Feelings, O My
Brother." This story also was often related by President
Grant, who loved the message and the lesson taught in
this composition. Again I turn to Brother Pyper's book
and quote extensively a story once well known, but not
now nearly so familiar:

> School thy feelings, O my brother
> Train thy warm, impulsive soul;
> Do not its emotions smother,
> But let wisdom's voice control.
>
> School thy feelings, there is power
> In the cool, collected mind;
> Passion shatters reason's tower,
> Makes the clearest vision blind.

School thy feelings, condemnation
Never pass on friend or foe.
Tho' the tide of accusation
Like the flood of truth may flow.

Hear defense before deciding
And a ray of light may gleam,
Showing thee what filth is hiding
Underneath the shallow stream.

Should affliction's acrid vial
Burst o'er thy unsheltered head,
School thy feelings to the trial,
Half its bitterness hath fled.

Art thou falsely, basely slandered?
Does the world begin to frown?
Guage thy wrath by wisdom's standard,
Keep thy rising anger down.

Rest thyself on this assurance:
Time's a friend to innocence;
And the patient, calm endurance
Wins respect and aids defense.

Noblest minds have finest feelings,
Quiv'ring strings a breath can move,
And the Gospel's sweet revealings,
Tune them with the key of love.

Hearts so sensitively moulded,
Strongly fortified should be,
Train'd to firmness and enfolded
In a calm tranquillity.

Wound not wilfully another;
Conquer haste with reason's might,
School thy feelings, sister, brother,
Train them in the path of right.

Brother Pyper explains that "in considering the poems of Charles W. Penrose one is impressed with the varying moods and emotions under which the author penned them." Brother Pyper quotes from President Penrose the trying circumstances related to the writing of this song, as related at the same social gathering when the General Authorities were guests of President Grant:

This hymn was not intended for singing. It was written for myself, about 1860, when I was in Birmingham, England, before I immigrated. I had been insidiously accused, not openly, but certain things had been said about me and my presidency of the Birmingham Conference, and particularly in relation to my family affairs and possessions. One thing connected with it might make the matter plain to you. When I went to Birmingham from Cheltenham—having previously been laboring in London—I had taken there a good deal of furniture and stuff belonging to my family that did not belong to the conference. It was intimated by one of the Elders from Zion that I was endeavoring to lay claim to the property that belonged to the Birmingham conference, and it touched me to the quick. I had labored then over ten years in the ministry, most of the time as traveling elder, literally without purse or scrip. I started that way and had continued, suffering a great many hardships and difficulties and trials that I need not refer to now, and this touched me right to the heart. I did not know how to bear it. Weltering under these feelings I sat down and wrote that little poem, right from my soul, and intended it for myself.

After I got it written my folks thought it ought to appear in the *Millennial Star*. So I sent it up to the Star and it was published. It was not set to any tune; I did not think about it being sung; in fact, I did not intend it for anybody but myself. However, I found it was quite applicable to others who had passed through similar experiences, and I thought it would be comforting to them. I was very pleased to know that it was a great comfort to President Brigham Young when he was under arrest. He later told me that he had it read to him several times when he had a deputy marshal guarding him in his house.

The words and origins of these two songs reveal the sensitive nature and love of God and his fellowmen of this giant among Latter-day Saint leaders.

President Penrose was an outstanding missionary. He served three missions in his native land during which he was active in assisting editorially with the *Millennial Star*. He also wrote many articles on the Church for London newspapers. While he was away on these missions, his articles appeared frequently in the *Star* and at home in Salt Lake City in the *Deseret News.*

While in Ogden, in 1877, he was asked by President Brigham Young to come to Salt Lake City to become editor-in-chief of the *Deseret News.* He held that position almost continuously, with a few intervals for missionary service and other editorial work with the *Ogden Junction* and the *Salt Lake Herald,* until 1907, three years after his call to the apostleship. At that time he returned again to England to succeed President Grant as president of the European Mission. Again his wide influence as preacher, teacher, editor, and writer was felt strongly not only in England but throughout all of Europe where he traveled constantly. He was the first apostle of the Church to visit any part of the world above the Arctic Circle.

President Penrose came home in 1910 and the next year was named second counselor in the First Presidency to President Joseph F. Smith, the prophet who had called him to be an apostle in 1904. He was sustained as second counselor also to President Grant in 1918, and advanced to first counselor in 1921 at the age of 89. When he died in May 1925, he was several months past his ninety-third birthday, having lived longer than any previous General Authority of the Church. His age was later exceeded only by the ages of President David O. McKay and President Joseph Fielding Smith. President McKay was four months past his ninety-sixth birthday when he died in January 1970, and President Smith died just two weeks before his ninety-sixth birthday, in July 1972.

PRESIDENT ANTHONY W. IVINS

I have often said that I considered President

Anthony W. Ivins one of the most unusual men I have ever known. He was literally a product of the rough and harshly demanding life of the pioneer west, but in every way he was a refined and true gentleman. He had very little scholastic learning, and yet he had unusual learning and scholarship. An educated man is described as one well rounded on every side of his nature. He exemplified this definition.

President Ivin's training came from personal experiences and from reading. He sometimes made the remark that there was not a mountain of any consequence that he had not climbed, nor a river of any size whose banks he had not traversed; there was not a country he had not visited, nor a city of any size he had not toured—*all in books!* He was a great student, and reading and study were a constant pursuit.

His language and speech were the best. He was at home with the millionaire, the aristocrat, the pioneer, and the Indian. As a boy growing up in southern Utah and northern Arizona, he played with the Indian boys and could most often beat them at horseback riding, shooting the bow and arrow, and other games.

The Indian people had the highest regard for President Ivins both as a friend and as an influential associate. To demonstrate their regard, a group of Indians came to Temple Square dressed in their finest regalia and between general conference sessions met President Ivins on the grounds south of the Tabernacle. As their friend stepped forward, one of the braves came from the circle and placed upon President Ivins a beautifully beaded buckskin vest. Their true regard for him was manifest in the beaded inscription on the back of the vest: "Tony Ivins, he no cheat."

When President Grant called President Ivins into
the First Presidency as a counselor in March 1921,
he not only paid tribute to a worthy cousin, but also
brought to his side a trusted lifelong friend, confidant, and associate. On one of his frequent trips
to St. George, Utah, President Grant was reminiscing
before his dictaphone, as he frequently did. He said:

> When President Brigham Young was in St. George on a par-
> ticular trip, he picked out a site to build a cotton factory at nearby
> Washington. My uncle, Israel Ivins, who was a surveyor and who
> had surveyed all of the southern Utah country, surveyed for a
> canal—or more properly speaking a large creek—to carry the water
> to run the water wheel at the cotton factory. My cousin, Anthony
> Ivins, was at one end of the surveyors chain at thirteen years of
> age, and I was at the other end at nine years.

Whenever opportunity presented over the many
years, as youngsters, as business associates, as
fellow members of the Council of the Twelve, and
then in the First Presidency, these two cousins were
the greatest of true friends. President Grant had ex-
plicit trust in his cousin "Tony."

President Ivins was a man of varied abilities
and interests. He was, first of all, a churchman, but
he was also a farmer, a stockgrower, a businessman, and, at the same time, one who understood
wildlife, animals, and human beings. He loved the
out-of-doors, and he had a great love of sports.
Ofttimes, when Salt Lake City was a part of the Pacific
Coast Baseball League and games were being played in
Salt Lake City, President Ivins would disappear from his
office in the afternoon without leaving any word as to
where he could be found. We in the office, however,
knew that he was at the baseball park.

He loved and understood horses better than anyone
I ever knew. On one occasion I spent some hours
with him and David P. Howells in Los Angeles,
visiting the stables where the best collection of
thoroughbred horses was being taken care of. As

we visited the many different horses with their owners and the name of the horse was mentioned, without hesitation President Ivins would name the ancestors— the sire and the mother, or dam.

Much of President Ivins' life was spend in the area about the Grand Canyon, including the Kaibab Forest. In 1928, when the Union Pacific Railroad built its huge Grand Canyon Lodge on the north rim of the canyon, it was fitting that President Ivins, then a counselor to President Grant, should be one of the principal speakers on the occasion of the formal opening. Two things resulted from that occasion. One was the introduction of his beloved counselor by President Heber J. Grant, in which the Church leader opened his heart and gave vent to his true feelings, and second, the response by President Ivins which will likely never be forgotten by those who heard it, or had occasion to read it in printed form as it was printed and distributed widely by the railroad officials.

Of President Ivins, President Grant said:

His life has been devoted to the highest ideals. In everything he has striven to do his best. In many things he has excelled.

As a young man he was the best baseball player, an adept with boxing gloves and the leading member of the local dramatic society. At one time he was acknowledged to be the best judge of horses and cattle in southern Utah. He was one of the most successful farmers, if not the most, in his section of the country. In civil affairs he has served the people in many capacities, always with distinction and integrity.

Not only is he a man of high moral courage, but he has proved himself on more than one occasion as a man of great physical courage and when serving as deputy sheriff he exhibited the fearlessness of his nature by arresting some of the most desperate characters in the country. He served several terms as a member of the Territorial Legislature, where he was regarded as one of the outstanding leaders. He was one of the framers of the state constitution. At one time his party offered him the nomination for governor of Utah, which he declined in order to accept a call to preside over the Mormon Colonies in Mexico.

While in Mexico he was on friendly terms with President Diaz, and in the last interview they had together President Diaz said to him, "There is no man in all the Republic of Mexico that I could enjoy doing business with more than you, Mr. Ivins."

In Church affairs he has also held many positions of honor, until today he stands second only to the president of the Church. Besides occupying these positions in the civil and religious life of the community, Mr. Ivins has developed into a successful business man, banker and merchant.

He is withal one of the most tender-hearted, forgiving and charitable men that it has ever been my good fortune to associate with. He is a lover of nature, of flowers, of beauty. He loves his fellowmen. He loves his horse, his dog, his gun, his fishing rod, and the mountains and forests, and the great outdoors.

The railroad officials, printing his speech for distribution, made this brief written account.

Mr. Ivins first saw the Grand Canyon country more than fifty-three years ago, and he has been a resident of it or neighbor to it ever since. He knows it—its people and their history, its wild life, its many colorful aspects—as few men do, and in his speech there on the brink of the canyon in the assembly room of the new lodge, this knowledge was distilled into prose poetry which gave a rare insight into the country.

Some of the comments of President Ivins show the true nature of the great leader as well as reveal his love for the great outdoors, which did so much in the sculpturing of his character. He said:

Roads made by men thread the world. We travel over them now on bands of steel, in luxurious motor cars, or through the air. Only yesterday our roads were mere trails, blazed by fearless intrepid men through unknown forests, over snowclad mountains, and across trackless deserts. The romance and tragedy of these old trails will never be told or written. It cannot be because the men who made unrecorded history over these devious ways have long since gone to tread the paths of another world, leaving little or no recorded history behind them.

Later in the same address he said:

It was in this environment that my early life was spent. I, too, became a tender of flocks and herds, first for others and later for myself, and it was under these circumstances, in constant association with men of like occupation, that the ideals and aspirations which have governed my life were formed. They were men of few words, these silent riders of the hills and plains, men of unsurpassed courage, but with hearts as tender as the hearts of women where acts of mercy and service were required, as often was the case. Profoundly religious, they held in reverential respect the religions of others. Not many audible prayers were said by them, but when the day's work was finished and the blankets spread down for the night, many silent petitions went up to the Throne of Grace in gratitude for blessings received and others desired.

Speaking of his beloved canyon he said:

The canyon below us and the mountain above have witnessed scenes more pathetic, more tragic than those told by any book maker. The trees, the grass, the animals, and the living springs of water teach lessons which cannot be taught in any university where the student has not had personal contact with them.

Such a man was this spiritual giant—so strong, yet so tender of heart and so compassionate with his fellowmen. Many a person came to see President Ivins and walked away with a small loan. None of them did he turn away.

President Ivins liked to sit at his own typewriter and compose his own letters and notes for sermons. It was with difficulty that we could get him to let us help. On one such occasion he wrote about the United Order in Orderville, Utah. It was a situation and experience with which he was familiar, and his comments have great historical significance.

I think the history of the United Order in Orderville ought to be preserved. It is the most remarkable history of the kind that will be in the records of the Church. It was the most successful effort of that kind that has ever been made since the Church was organized, and it was not a failure—it was a success. I went to Orderville with Erastus Snow when he disorganized the Order. They owned the entire Kaibab mountain and were securing all the farms in that country. They had their own sheep herds, their own factories to make their wool into cloth; they had their own cattle and tanneries to tan the hides from which to make shoes. It looked as though they would absorb the whole country if something was not done to stop it—the people of other communities became jealous of them. I asked President Snow the reason for discontinuing the order there, and he said they were ahead of the times, that we could not have the United Order in one community of the Church when everybody else was out, and everybody could not get in there. That was the argument. I worked in it and I want to say I never regretted a moment the hard work I did in the United Order. It came the nearest to the ideal plan which is bound to be established in this Church and which is just as sure to come as that we are here. It may not be the same plan, but it will be the same general thought; and when I think of Orderville and hear of it, I think that the record of what was done by that people should be preserved.

President Ivins was a constant student of the scriptures and was perhaps as well informed about the Book of Mormon, especially, as was anyone in the Church. His many sermons are real contributions to the literature and doctrinal discussions of the Church. In them he has left a rich heritage. It has been said that "it is intellect and emotion expanded in every direction that give the true title to greatness." Judged by this measure, President Ivins was a great man. It is one's conduct in life that gives a correct indication of one's education, not the colleges in which he has matriculated nor the degrees he has received. Life was this man's master teacher.

Anthony W. Ivins was ordained an apostle on October 6, 1907, during the presidency of Joseph F. Smith. President Grant called him as second counselor in March 1921, and in May 1925 he was called to be first counselor in the First Presidency.

As further affirmation of my oft-repeated claim that the Lord knew and called these great men to their positions long before they were born in mortality, I repeat in closing a typical, practical comment from President Grant, concerning the call to Mexico of President Ivins:

I was feeling as "blue" financially as I ever did in my life when my cousin, Anthony W. Ivins, was called to go to Mexico.

He had been marvelously successful in operating ranches. He had a little ranch worth $50,000 which we owned between us, which for years had paid 25% dividends every year regularly, and the panic had come on and institutions that I had money in and in which I had borrowed money failed. That ranch was paying 6% interest on $50,000 of my debts. I was sitting in the temple, heartbroken, although I was one of the committee that nominated him, because I felt impressed that he was needed in Mexico and that the Lord wanted him to be there. It came to me as plainly as though the voice of the Lord had declared it, "You need not feel sad because your cousin is going to Mexico; he is going exactly where the Lord wants him to go, and you shall have the exquisite joy of welcoming him back into this room of the temple as an apostle of this last dispensation."

PRESIDENT CHARLES W. NIBLEY

The often-heard characterization of being a self-made man was probably more rightfully earned by President Charles W. Nibley than by any other who achieved high leadership as a member of the First Presidency of the Church. Born in a coal mining town in Scotland and living almost in the depths of poverty, Charles W. Nibley achieved the distinction of being one of the powerful and most capable spiritual, industrial, and financial leaders of western America of his day.

This all came about because of the gospel of Jesus Christ, and President Nibley never lost sight of that fact. He was born in Hunterfield, about six miles south of Edinburgh, Scotland, on February 5, 1849. When the gospel found his folks in Scotland, they were living in a two-room rock house. His father was working in the coal mine nearby, earning three shillings a day and carrying coal out of the mine on his back.

President Nibley said that he never knew the day when he lived there in that rock house that he had enough to eat, mostly porridge and the like. On one

occasion many years later, President Nibley, speaking
to his children in front of that two-room rock home,
said, "I want you to know that the only thing in the
world that would have pulled us out of this condition
was the gospel. If it had not been for the Church
we would no doubt be living in that house today.
All that we are and all that we ever will be we owe to
the Mormon Church, and do not forget it."

It is said of Thomas Carlyle that he loved
Ecclefechan, the little village in Scotland where he
was born and reared; that he preferred to be buried
there rather than in Westminster Abbey. I am sure
that President Nibley also had a great love for the
land of his birth, and he loved the writings of
Carlyle and Sir Walter Scott, but I am sure he never
had the longing to return to that land to make his
home or to be buried. Instead he had an oft-expressed
appreciation to the Lord that the gospel had found
his parents and himself in that humble village of
hardworking coal miners and made it possible for
him to come to Utah and America and enjoy the
blessings of freedom and opportunity.

After hearing the gospel in 1844, the Nibley
family took several years to achieve, with hard
struggle and sacrifice, their goal of coming to America.
Meanwhile a branch of the Church had been organized
in Hunterfield, and the father, James Nibley, had
served as the branch president. In 1855 they
finally left Scotland, crossing the Atlantic in the
steerage of a sailing vessel. Their finances would take
them no farther than Rhode Island, where they remained for the next five years working in woolen
mills.

Charles W. was a lad of eleven years when the
family started in 1860 on their trip across the plains
to Salt Lake City. They settled almost immediately
in Wellsville, Cache County. The Scottish immigrant

boy herded cows to help the meager family income, and he later related that his parents did not have the means to buy clothes for him; he managed with a piece of burlap wrapped around him instead of pants.

I relate these few experiences of his early life to show the humble beginning of the career of one who became one of the noble and great among the leadership of the Church. He became a man of great wealth, literally an industrial giant, with his holdings and influence reaching throughout Utah, Idaho, Oregon, and California. Yet never did he falter in his devotion to the Church. He gave liberally of his talents and means to promote the work of the Lord. He was an organizer of railroads and became a railroad president. He was one of the principal founders and organizers of the LeGrande Sugar Company, which later merged into the Amalgamated Sugar Company. The lumber business that he helped to organize extended into many parts of Oregon and into California.

As a result of these varied enterprises, President Nibley was a man of affluence as well as wide influence. When the Saints in eastern Oregon and western Idaho were organized into the Union Stake in 1901, Charles W. Nibley became a counselor in the stake presidency.

In 1906 President Nibley, with others of his family, traveled to Europe with President Joseph F. Smith. This was the first of numerous travels to many parts of the world that President Nibley was subsequently to make with presidents of the Church, both President Smith and President Heber J. Grant. Some of these trips were made in connection with selecting sites for temples in Hawaii, Arizona, Canada, and for dedications of these temples when they were completed.

However, these subsequent trips were made by President Nibley in a new official assignment of Church leadership. He had become Presiding Bishop of the Church, appointed to this important post in December 1907 by President Smith. Perhaps in no other Church position could the business acumen and financial experiences of President Nibley be used more effectively than as Presiding Bishop, wherein he had control of the tithes and funds of the Church. It was under his administration that the tithing system of the Church was changed to a cash basis and the use of tithing scrip became a thing of the past.

Many things could be written of President Nibley's long and effective service as Presiding Bishop of the Church from 1907 until his call as second counselor to President Grant in May 1925. At that time, President Anthony W. Ivins was moved to first counselor to succeed the late Charles W. Penrose, and President Nibley filled the vacancy. This was the first change in personnel of the First Presidency I had experienced, and I soon learned that the Lord always has in preparation someone to appoint to fill a vacancy among the General Authorities. The appointment of President Nibley was further evidence to me of the divine influence of the Lord in inspiring his prophets to make these selections. It was well known by their close associates that, while President Grant and Bishop Nibley were united in their church relationship and presiding positions, they were frequently in conflict in their business relationship, particularly in regard to the sugar industry. This conflict arose from the leadership the two had in competing companies, President Grant with the Utah-Idaho Sugar Company and President Nibley with the Amalgamated Sugar Company.

During the more than six years that President Nibley served as a counselor to President Grant,

however, there was never a question of his loyalty
and devotion to his prophet-leader, and his contribution to this high office was of great magnitude.
He was a wonderful counselor, and he and President
Grant and President Ivins always worked together
with the utmost harmony and love.

President Nibley, while serving as one of the
three high priests who presided over the Church,
never did become one of the Twelve Apostles. In this
respect he ranked with several others in Church
history, including Sidney Rigdon, Daniel H. Wells, and
John R. Winder.

I have always had a personal admiration and
love for President Nibley. He was a noble character.
He never had the opportunity for formal schoolroom
education, but he became a very well-informed man,
educated in the important things of life. He had a
strong familiarity with the writings of Shakespeare,
and he loved them as he did the writings of Thomas
Carlyle. His life reflected a refinement of character
second to none. He was a great organizer and a
very astute and successful businessman.

One thing I remember most fondly of President
Nibley was his outstanding sense of humor. He
became known and appreciated as one of the most
able of speakers, his talks always practical but
punctuated with humorous stories and incidents to
illustrate his points. I have known few if any men
who had such a wonderful supply of stories and who
used them so appropriately as did President Nibley.

Although Scottish by birth, he was never "scotch"
in the sense that we sometimes think of people of
his nationality as far as money is concerned. On
one occasion when his finances were good, he gave
Nibley Park to the Church. This now popular Salt
Lake City golf course was at that time considered
to be worth a great amount of money. On another

occasion, which demonstrated his practical sense of humor, he gave once—and I cannot remember the year—to his friends and associates an attractive Christmas card that was good also for the next two years. It read, and I'll have to substitute the years, "Merry Christmas for 1928, 1929, and 1930." The card was covered with colorful Scotch plaid.

There came a time when President Nibley's finances declined very greatly, but he was never heard to complain in the least because of it.

I shall always be grateful to him for his kindness and consideration of me personally. President Grant was a very active man in those years, and seldom, if ever, did he spend a Sunday at home. He was always visiting wards and stakes, where he dedicated meetinghouses and preached to the people. It had become my lot to drive the car for him nearly always when he made these trips. President Nibley would occasionally say to President Grant, "Heber, don't you think you should leave Joseph at home with his family tomorrow?" And, of course, the suggestion having been made, President Grant always followed it and someone else drove him on those occasions, and I did enjoy the weekend with my family.

I remember on the occasion when my third child was born, President Grant suggested (I was told) that I be given a twenty-five dollar raise in monthly salary. President Nibley suggested, in which President Ivins immediately enjoined, that I be given instead a fifty-dollar-a-month increase. That was approved unanimously. In those days a fifty-dollar-a-month increase was a mighty big raise.

As a man of many accomplishments, of unusual personal enterprise, of exceptional devotion and dedication to the Church, President Nibley was always humble, practical, and very approachable.

He had a great love for his family, and there was nothing he would not do for them—sometimes perhaps, as is the case with many of us, overdoing the matter. I respected him for all his achievements and service, but I appreciated him most of all for his genuineness, humanness, loyalty, and friendship.

PRESIDENT J. REUBEN CLARK, JR.

President J. Reuben Clark, Jr., came into the First Presidency as second counselor to President Grant in 1933, when he succeeded Charles W. Nibley in that position. President Anthony W. Ivins, who was the first counselor, remarked to President Grant a few days after President Nibley's passing, "I don't know who in the world we can get to take President Nibley's place." President Grant answered immediately, "I know just the man." "Who is it?" asked President Ivins. President Grant replied, "J. Reuben Clark, Jr." President Ivins said, "Just the man!"

President Clark was a native of Grantsville, Utah, where he was born on September 1, 1871. Grantsville was once described by a biographer of President Clark as one of those pioneer Utah towns which "were also melting pots of many nationalities . . . and where representatives of many lands rubbed shoulders in the toil of subduing the desert. Everyone had to work from childhood up or starve. . . . Grantsville and the towns like it produced men great before God and powerful before their fellowmen."

Such a man I found J. Reuben Clark, Jr., to be. He loved to work and accepted readily the ever-present challenge to achieve. It was said of him that "he was taught the dignity and necessity

of work and had practiced it all of his life. He
loved learning. He would have knowledge and
would pay the price for it."

This thirst for knowledge, coupled with an intelligence and ability well above the average,
eventually took him into high places in the government of his country. It was in these circles that he
was best known when the call to the First Presidency
came. He had acquired fame as an international
lawyer and was the author of legal documents
and decisions that still formulate national and
international policy.

Before he went to the East to pursue his higher
educational degrees, he was a schoolteacher, first
in Heber City, then at the Salt Lake Business College,
and for one year he was the principal of the Branch
Normal School (now the College of Southern Utah)
at Cedar City. But the thirst for knowledge and
the challenge to achieve took him to Columbia
University. With his wife, the former Luacine Savage,
and two small children, he went off to New York
to study law. The coveted LL.B. degree was won
in 1906 when he was 35 years of age.

His achievement at school was such that he
stepped from the campus to the United States
State Department as assistant solicitor under Elihu
Root. Achievements at the height of his professional
career brought him such posts as Undersecretary
of State and as a major in the army during World
War I, assigned to the office of the Judge Advocate
General. In recognition of his war service he was
awarded three silver chevrons and the Distinguished
Service Medal. Among other notable services he
rendered was his service as an assistant for several
years to Ambassador Dwight W. Morrow in Mexico.
Then for several years he was himself ambassador.

Such was his national and international service

that he filled with distinction special commissions and assignments from seven presidents of the United States.

Withal his remarkable career in government and world affairs, his loyalty to the Church was his foremost characteristic. In New York, Washington, D.C., Mexico City, or wherever his assignments took him, his home was a center of church activity, not alone for his family, but for other Latter-day Saints of his acquaintance as well. His associates knew of his devotion to the Church and of his great faith. He was ever loyal under all circumstances to the principles of the restored gospel. Little known was his profound study of the gospel and especially of the life and teachings of the Savior.

When President Grant called him into the First Presidency, Brother Clark was serving as U.S. Ambassador to Mexico. President Grant communicated his wishes to Brother Clark by correspondence, and the call to the First Presidency was accepted. However, it was some months before President Clark could make the necessary adjustments to come to Salt Lake City. I recall that he had been offered very lucrative employment in the East, but he declined and always said that he never had any ambition to make a lot of money.

Too much cannot be said of President Clark's great experience and ability as a servant of the people in civil, governmental, and diplomatic affairs. That experience gave him training that proved of unlimited benefit to the Church. His knowledge and understanding of the English language was unusual. It can truly be said of him that he knew the meaning of words and how to use them. He had a brilliant mind, and his memory did not seem to dim with age.

President Grant had but very limited acquaintance

with Brother Clark when he chose him to be a
counselor, but certainly time proved that he made
no mistake and that his selection was inspired of
the Lord.

During the last five years of President Grant's
life, he was in ill health, and President Clark was
required to carry a great deal of responsibility,
as first counselor in the First Presidency. No one
could have been more considerate of his superiors
than was President Clark. At no time did he take
upon himself the responsibility of making decisions
or taking actions of importance, but always he
consulted with President Grant and the · other
counselor, President McKay, to ascertain their feelings
in the matter. President Grant had implicit confidence
in President Clark's judgment, and they had a deep
love for each other. When President Grant passed
away and the First Presidency was reorganized,
President George Albert Smith chose the same
counselors to assist him that served President
Grant: J. Reuben Clark, Jr., and David O. McKay.
President Smith also had the utmost confidence and
love for President Clark and leaned heavily upon
his support.

When President McKay became president of the
Church, he chose as his counselors Stephen L. Richards
and J. Reuben Clark, Jr. President Clark had served
two presidents, President Grant and President
Smith, as first counselor in the First Presidency and
had given an invaluable service in that capacity
to those great men. With a courage that has seldom
been equaled, I am sure, in Church administration,
he now accepted the position of second counselor
with the statement, "It is not where one serves
but how." At President McKay's request he presented, to the various divisions of priesthood
assembled in the Tabernacle, the General Authori-

ties of the Church for their sustaining vote, in each instance reading the names of the First Presidency in the new order, and he did a masterful job of it. Be it said to his credit, no man could have been more loyal, faithful, and devoted to his file leader than was President Clark to the day of his death. There was a deep bond of affection between those two men.

Upon the death of President Stephen L Richards in 1959, President Clark again became the first counselor in the First Presidency of the Church.

Perhaps few men have been closer to each other than were President Clark and I. He many times orally and in writing spoke appreciatively and affectionately of me. He was a true friend, one from whom I learned great and valuable lessons and one for whom I had the utmost admiration and affection. He trusted me with his confidences; in fact, he revealed to me the innermost thoughts of his heart. Similarly, I kept very little, if anything, from him. True friends are rare indeed, and such a friend was President Clark. It is a matter of happiness and satisfaction to have a friend like him. I am sure that when the time comes for us to meet beyond the veil, that friendship will continue, and I hope it will be everlasting.

"Perhaps few men were closer to each other than I was to President J. Reuben Clark, Jr."

No one can testify more than I to the great service this man performed for the Church. He truly magnified his position in the First Presidency and vitalized the statement he made in conference at the time of the death of President Smith and the reorganization of the First Presidency, that it is not where one serves, but how he serves, that is important.

As is perhaps quite generally known, President Clark served as second counselor to President Grant for a year and a half as a high priest and was not ordained an apostle until October 11, 1934, when, at the time of filling the vacancy in the Quorum of the Twelve caused by the calling of David O. McKay to be the second counselor in the First Presidency, President Grant called President Clark to be an apostle, and he was so ordained by President Grant and set apart as a member of the Quorum of the Twelve. Inasmuch as President Grant wished him to continue as his first counselor, Brother Alonzo A. Hinckley was chosen to be a member of the Twelve, filling the vacancy thus created.

President Clark had a remarkable sense of humor, and always had a story or experience to tell to illustrate a point.

He was also very generous. His hobby was his farm in his native Grantsville, Utah, and he owned large farm interests. When he had time to spare, he loved to spend it on the farm. His farm was not intended to be a money-making business, but he seemed to have an innate love for the country and things connected with farm life. He took great joy in using the products of his farm to bless his friends. Never did a year pass that he didn't arrange to have meat prepared, such as beef, pork, or lamb, to give to his friends. He seemed always to receive much enjoyment from contributing to the happiness of others. He took pride in a tribute paid him by Dwight Morrow, who at the time was U.S. Ambassador to Mexico and by whom Brother Clark was employed as counsel. "Mr. Clark," he said, "I have never known a man who thought less of the dollar than you." The tribute was well deserved—he was a man with a proper understanding of values, and with him the material things of life sank into oblivion when compared to the eternal values.

In answer to my question as to how well he knew President Grant at the time he was called to be second counselor in the First Presidency, President Clark told me the following:

I do not know that he knew me at all except that I had met him perhaps a half dozen times in my life. Sister Clark and I came into the office before I went to Mexico, and I asked him for and received a blessing. This was when I went as Ambassador to Mexico in October 1930. I had no acquaintance with him practically. I asked him once how he came to choose me, and he said, "Oh, I had heard you speak." I said, "Where?" Well, he was indefinite. He said, "Well, I knew your grandfather," and after I came into the Presidency he said, "As long as you live, your grandfather will never be dead." He then repeated the previously mentioned conversation with President Ivins relative to his selection for the First Presidency.

President Clark was an ordained seventy at the time he was chosen and had been for a number of years. He was also a member of the YMMIA general board.

President Clark also said:

When I was a very young child lying in bed in the room where my mother and father were, President Grant was present, he at the time being the president of Tooele Stake, and he was in the room talking to father and mother. This was in Grantsville.

A few of us kids (there were Oscar Johnson, Orlando Barrus, Jimmie Williams, and two or three others) used to go out either on the 4th or 24th of July (I have forgotten which) in the morning and celebrate. On one occasion we had a lumber box wagon and a four horse team. We got up before daylight and went around serenading. Jimmie Ratcliffe was the drummer, and the rest of us had flutes or some sort of instrument, and we played a few tunes—I do not remember what—mostly by ear.

On one occasion I was chosen as the reader of the day, which meant that at the celebration (I suppose it was the 4th of July) I would read probably the Declaration of Independence and then read the toasts. They would hold a morning meeting. On this occasion I was up there and had done my initial reading, and then it came my turn to read the toasts. I was about 14, I assume. I was up there—just imagine a 14-year-old kid—and I stood there waiting for the toasts to come to me to be read. Francis M. Lyman was there on the stand participating in the celebration. When it came time for his toast he said, "I always read my own toasts," and that ended my toast reading, and I stood there, country-bumpkin as I was. I remember my father saying afterwards, "I would have given anything if I had been near enough to you to pull you down from that stand." That is the only experience I had with a General Authority all during my youthful life.

The day Brother Grant was appointed President of the Tooele Stake he was in my father's home, but I do not remember it.

As previously mentioned, it was in December 1931 that President Grant wrote Brother Clark telling him of his calling to be a counselor in the First Presidency. Brother Clark left Mexico in February 1933, went to Washington and made his report as ambassador, and then came to Salt Lake City where he was sustained second counselor on April 6, 1933. He remained in Salt Lake City until October 1933, when he went back to Washington to serve on the Foreign Bondholders Council, and then in early 1934 he went to Uruguay to the seventh Pan-American Conference of all American Nations in Montevideo. Cordell Hull was the head of the United States delegation, but he did not remain all the time, and President Clark became the head of the U.S. delegation.

The *New York Times* of Sunday, October 23, 1923, said of President Clark, when he was appointed Undersecretary of State under President Coolidge:

He has had a part both officially and as an unofficial advisor to American leaders, in the formulation of our international relations. He was at the elbow of Knox (Senator of Penna.) during the historic conflict in the Senate over the League of Nations.

Mr. Clark was assistant to Charles Evans Hughes during the Washington Conference for the Limitation of Armament and as such sat with Hughes during the many private discussions with the heads of the delegations representing the two other major sea powers—Great Britain and Japan.

[He] went to Mexico with Dwight Morrow as his special counsel.

Thus Mr. Clark had a share in preparing the way for the settlement which Morrow finally made with President Calles. This was on a controversial oil problem.

In the Taft administration, Taft and Knox took the load in applying a new principle to the conduct of our foreign relations. Under this principle the U.S. was prepared to use its diplomatic machinery, so far as it legitimately could, to protect American property and interests abroad. The question was "what right have Congress and the President, either under the Constitution or under the accepted practices of international law, to land troops or marines on foreign soil when American lives and property are jeopardized?" This question confronted President Taft and his Secretary of State, and they proceeded to formulate the foreign policy of the Administration.

Knox asked Clark to make an historical study of our intervention policy. The result was an exhaustive memorandum on the "Right of the U.S. to Protect its Citizens in Foreign Countries by Landing Forces."

The survey he made was the first and only thorough analysis of the kind ever made.

President Woodrow Wilson appointed him general counsel for the U.S. before the American-British Claims Commission.

When the U.S. entered the war Provost Marshall Crowder, the man charged with the administration of the Selective Draft act, employed Clark who had been commissioned an officer in the Judge Advocate General's department as one of his assistants. As a special assistant to the Attorney General he also made an analysis of all the war legislation passed by Congress. In 1922 he received the D.S.M. for his service.

He was offered $100,000 a year by one of the great corporations of America when he left Mexico as Ambassador.

Mr. Morrow paid him as his advisor almost as much as Mr. Morrow received from the government as Ambassador, and he received $75,000 a year.

He was told by the chairman of one of the great banks in New York that if he came to New York he could write his own ticket.

But instead, this great and good man chose to honor his priesthood, to enter a yet greater avenue of service to his fellowmen by devoting the remainder of his life to building up the kingdom of God.

My association with President Clark was one of the sweetest and most enjoyable that two men could have together. Seldom did a day pass that we weren't together for hours, giving attention to correspondence and taking care of matters of importance to the Church. He was like a father to me, and he often said he looked upon me as a son. I knew his sorrows and his joys. Everyone seems to have need for someone with whom to share his thoughts, his joys, his disappointments, his successes, and his sorrows. Those experiences were very frequently confidential and of a nature that are held in memory but cannot be revealed to others. Too much can never be written nor told about the greatness and goodness of this man.

President Clark was always very solicitous of the personal welfare of his many friends, and I often became aware of his feelings toward me. Frequently these expressions were put in writing, especially as he responded, as he always did, to a Christmas or birthday remembrance. These notes of his are among my treasures, and I select the following one as typical and present it in humility just to demonstrate the boundless capacity of this good man to show gratitude and encouragement. This note my wife and I received under date of December 26, 1959, just two years before his death in October 1961:

Dear Joseph and Norma:

Your remembrance of me at this Christmas Time was, of course, something that made me very happy. But you have always remembered me, which made me happy in the past, and I would have been disappointed if I had not been remembered this time, and yet I know the affection, the loyalty, and the devotion, Joseph, which you have manifested over the years, and without which I could not have done what I have done, and I have been most grateful to know that Norma was always behind you, helping in all ways that she could in the great work which you are doing there in the Presidency's office.

God bless both of you abundantly and give you always a full portion of the health and the strength which you wish and which you deserve, and give you peace of mind and comfort of body....

May the many endowments which the Lord has given to you, Joseph, never fail you so long as you live, and may you always be able, as I am sure you will, while there is still strength in your body, to perform the duties of the great office which is yours.

The office will miss you, Joseph, when you are gone, but I hope and pray that that missing will not come for many, many years.

As I have said to you in the past, so I say to you again, there is nothing that I can say in commendation more than I have tried to say in the past and more than you deserve.

God bless you both always, and yours, and give you happiness and joy in your family relationship and be with you with His Spirit and His testimony and the knowledge that you have, so long as you live.

With love,

[Signed] J. Reuben Clark Jr.

P.S. I got so concerned in trying to tell you once again a little of what I thought of both of you that I forgot to thank you for the beautiful assortment of jams which you sent me. They will prove to be delicious. Thank you so much, they are of the finest quality, I am sure.

P.P.S. And for the Swedish cake that Norma sent to me, I am looking forward to its sampling.

In yet another note, two years earlier, he had this to say about our treasured association:

I have well-nigh exhausted the good adjectives I know in trying to express to Joseph my appreciation for his work. Joseph is a humble but great soul. He has worked over the years with great and unselfish devotion, taking no thought of himself, but only of those with whom he works, and of his work itself. I am more his debtor than I can ever repay in this life, and I must wait until Eternity to try to show him my gratitude, my respect, and my love.

Joseph, may the Lord be with you in the future as in the past, and He has blessed you greatly in the past. And Norma, you are good for helping to keep him well and strong and carrying on. May the Lord bless you in your great labors for the Church, too.

I cannot resist the temptation to record what to Norma, my wife, and me, was a very sacred occasion.

It was a Christmas party during the Christmas season. President Clark had invited us to come to his home and spend the evening with him and members of his family, as also some close friends. This was at a time when he was advanced in years; in fact, not very long before his passing, and he was showing the effects of weakness and poor health.

We were happy to go and it was an evening that impressed itself upon our memories in a manner that we shall never forget. He spent the evening in his library upstairs, was unable to come downstairs to mingle with his guests. Sister Anderson and I, with his secretary, Rowena Miller, and one or two other friends, visited with him in his library. He asked his secretary to bring to him from his safe a pen written letter that President Grand had written him asking him to serve as his counselor in the First Presidency. As he read the letter to us, tears ran down his cheeks and his voice choked with emotion. He explained that he did not reveal the contents of this letter to his wife or other members of the family for two or three days as he pondered its contents. He was at the time American Ambassador to Mexico.

He of course answered in the affirmative, but his duties in connection with his government service somewhat delayed his assumption of complete responsibility in the office of the First Presidency, but when he did give his full attention to his new duties he most certainly more than made up for any restrictions on his time previously.

On the occasion above referred to we were with him

for a couple of hours as he reminisced and told the story of his life. He wanted to share these treasured experiences with his closest friends.

President Clark was an assiduous worker. When others played, he was burning the midnight oil, studying, writing, or otherwise devoting himself to the service to which he had been assigned. I remember on one occasion visiting a businessmen's club in Washington where he had spent many hours in his earlier years while in the government service. He showed me the tables where men who lived there as he had done spent many hours playing cards. He did not criticize them, but he said he had had no time for such things. I think that all his life he worked and read and studied during the late hours of the night and the early hours of the morning.

President Clark had an extensive library, collected over the years of his schooling and professional activities. Prominent in his library were books on international law, but he also had one of the largest collections of books and writings on the life of the Savior. Study of the scriptures and particularly the life and teachings of the Master were of the utmost interest to him, and he acquired many valuable and rare books in the field.

This theme predominated most of his many sermons and writings, including published books, during his many years in the First Presidency.

Since much of his life prior to the time he was called to assist President Grant was devoted to governmental and diplomatic service, his talents and abilities along those lines manifested themselves to a great degree in his Church work. Statements that he wrote, letters that he dictated, and sermons that he preached were masterpieces of wisdom, inspiration, and rhetoric.

President Clark had a great love and admiration for President Grant as an individual, as well as a prophet, and this respect was made evident in the following tribute paid by him to President Grant on May 10, 1941, when the latter was introduced into the Union Pacific Railroad Old Timers' Club:

What the world most needs today are the qualities .he so richly has for his own; a knowledge that God lives and directs the affairs of men; that the lowly Carpenter of Nazareth is indeed the Messiah, the Savior of the world; that the righteous life is the way to joy here and to salvation hereafter; that honor and truth are beyond price; that honesty, industry, thrift, charity, generosity, chastity, love for fellowmen, unselfishness are the precious pearls that strung together make the noble character; and that avarice, greed, immorality, ambition, idleness, false witness corrupt the people and debase the men. All these virtues, every one of them he has. They are part of the warp and woof of his life. The vices he cast aside while he was yet a mere boy.

President Grant has been a most successful man of affairs in a large sense; he is a builder of commonwealths. In business he has had his feet always on the ground. He has been hard headed but not selfish. His mind has never entertained the area of impracticable plans and schemes of the theorists or the so-called idealists. He has known true economic values. He has been bounteously generous but he has never been blinded to the true value and purpose of the time.

And all this has been but a part, the smaller part of his full to brimming life. So, I want to speak tonight of the other, the larger part of his life, for along with all this dealing in matters temporal he has been a God-fearing man of the loftiest spirituality, believing even as the little child believes in the power of the Lord and the Lord's willingness to answer prayer. It is this spirituality which has led and dominated this man of affairs through his whole business career. He boldly asserts that time and time again the Lord has blessed him, has answered his prayers in his own behalf, in behalf of his family, of his friends, and of his people. He knows those things with all the certainty that he knows that he lives. There is no doubt anywhere in his soul.

President Clark was a man possessed of greatness

of character. He was one who exemplified true Christian ideals, and at the same time he was a great American. We often discussed America's problems, and he understood and spoke out often in warning about the dangers of concentrating too much power in a central government. He once made a patriotic radio address on the subject "Why I Am an American." His message found its way into the *Congressional Record.* His faith in the divine source of American principles is summarized in the last two paragraphs of that message, which read:

I am an American because I firmly and earnestly believe that the Constitution is an inspired document designed by our Maker to set up a government which would make sure and secure the rights set forth in the Bill of Rights, and particularly the right of freedom of conscience and worship.

I am an American because I believe that the destiny of America is to be the abiding place of liberty and free institutions, and that its own practice and enjoyment of these blessings shall be to the world a beacon light which shall radiate its influence by peaceful means to the uttermost parts of the world, to the uplifting of all humanity.

His great role as a defender of the American Constitution was recognized in these words of tribute to President Clark in a resolution of respect from the board of directors of the Equitable Life Assurance Company on which he had served so long and well:

To him the Constitution of the United States was as sacred in safeguarding the liberties of this nation, as the Holy Scriptures are a guide to eternal life. He was considered as one of the ablest defenders of the Constitutional government and with forthright statesmanship never hesitated to condemn modern trends which have seemed to violate the basic concepts as written into the Constitution by the founding fathers.

On one occasion President Clark gave a Washington's Birthday dinner speech in Salt Lake City, sponsored by the Utah Society of Sons of the American Revolution. I conclude this chapter with the last

paragraph of that address, which I find not only
adds to the great Americanism of President Clark,
but shows his ability to express himself in a wonderful display of rhetoric and the commingling of his
great faith in God and outstanding patriotism. To
him the two were never separated.

On this occasion he said:

But my time is past. When the spirit of Washington broods
over our thoughts, we can but wish to crush out the treason
to our liberties, and free institutions, to human rights, which
seeks to find place in our fair land. We would become Crusaders
as of old, seeking to preserve from despoilment the holy dwelling-
place of our sacred treasure and heritage, our Federal Constitution.
Washington's kneeling in prayer in the crusted snow at Valley
Forge, with his freezing, starving men on every side, may be
but a fiction, but it typifies the spirit that held aloft the torch of
human rights and liberties through all those trying years, the
spirit that sifted out unholy ambition, materialism, theft, covetous-
ness, and civic selfishness from the hearts of men, that made
heroes of common clay. That spirit had its counterpart in
Franklin's proposal for prayer after days of fruitless wrangling
at the Constitutional Convention. Belief in and understanding of
the relationship between God and man, of man's dependence on
God, are the great needs of today, that the living spirit of Washington's America shall be fed, not starved. God grant that in his
infinite mercy, in his love for his erring children, that spirit of
Washington's America shall be fed, not starved. God grant that
in his infinite mercy, in his love for his erring children, that spirit
of belief and understanding may come to us of America ere
it is too late, and again enkindle in our souls the love of truth over
error, of freedom over slavery, of independence over dependence,
a reverence for human rights and free local self-government over
despotism and tyranny, that shall carry on this free people through
the gamut of unnumbered centuries yet to come.

SECTION TWO

Leadership of President George Albert Smith

4

President Smith,
A Man Who Loved All Men

President George Albert Smith was often characterized as the apostle and prophet of love. As I was privileged to know him for nearly 30 years, both as a member of the Council of the Twelve and as the president of the Church, I found this to be a most appropriate designation. Though he was president for but six years, they were eventful years, marked by unusual accomplishments seemingly involving to the utmost his love for all mankind and a spirit of goodwill.

As I look back on his accomplishments in his presidency, I am again, more than ever, impressed with the fact that the Lord raises up the right man to become his earthly prophet and leader to accomplish the special mission appropriate to the day and time.

The death of President Grant and the selection and sustaining of President Smith brought this humble secretary face to face with a new and awesome spiritual experience that I was to go through on other future occasions. With the death of the president, the First Presidency was then dissolved and the leadership of the Church throughout the world was assumed

President George Albert Smith, center, selected as his counselors the two who had served President Grant. Left is President J. Reuben Clark, Jr. and right is President David O. McKay.

by the Council of the Twelve, even though for a few short days. The manner in which the membership of the Twelve rallied behind George Albert Smith, their quorum president, sustaining him in every way during the funeral services of the deceased president, and the subsequent reorganization of the First Presidency permitted me to observe and sense the spirit of revelation as it rested mightily upon these brethren.

When that hour came during the solemn council meeting of the Twelve in the sacred atmosphere of the Salt Lake Temple, President Smith selected as his counselors the two men who had been serving as counselors to President Grant: J. Reuben Clark, Jr., and David O. McKay. They served him faithfully and devotedly throughout his full administration. These were faithful, dedicated, and strong men, men of inspiration—a great First Presidency.

I not only witnessed the unusual power of the unanimity of these brethren of the Twelve as they proceeded with the reorganization of the First Presidency, but I found myself rejoicing personally in what had been done. These two faithful counselors had served long and well in the previous presidency, and I had learned to love and appreciate them. I had known how heavily President Grant had leaned upon these two spiritual giants, and especially during the last years of his presidency when his health was not as robust.

I was to learn during the next six years also how much trust and confidence President Smith was to place in his counselors. Neither ever took advantage of that trust.

President Smith brought a rich personal heritage with him into his office of prophet, seer, and revelator—a heritage of birthright and of long and faithful service by his ancestors in the restored kingdom of God. He was born in Salt Lake City on April 4, 1870, a son of John Henry Smith. His father and grandfather, George A. Smith, had also served in the Council of the Twelve Apostles, and the two had also been counselors in the First Presidency.

Grandfather George A. Smith was a cousin of the Prophet Joseph Smith and was chosen one of the Twelve Apostles in 1839 during the lifetime of the Prophet. He later served as a counselor to President Brigham Young in the First Presidency. Father John Henry Smith was named a member of the Twelve in 1880 and later became a counselor to President Joseph F. Smith, sixth president of the Church.

President George Albert Smith was always proud of his ancestry, not alone for their service to the Church since its founding in 1830, but for their part

in the founding of the American commonwealth and
participation in the American Revolutionary War and
as defenders of the Constitution. President Smith
traced his ancestry to Edward Winslow, governor of
Plymouth Colony, who came to this land on the *May-
flower* in search of freedom and religious liberty.
His great-grandfather, John Smith, who was an uncle
of the Prophet Joseph, was Patriarch to the Church
and also the first president of the Salt Lake Stake.

President Smith said of his own father, "I have
never met a greater man." However, the fact that he
carried his grandfather's name also meant a great
deal to him. He knew this grandfather only as a child
some five years old before George A. Smith's death.
Bearing that name helped greatly in the forming of
President Smith's life's pattern. "That has meant
much to me to have that sacred name to take care of,"
he said often as he described what to him was a
sacred experience:

One day while being seriously ill, I lost consciousness of my
surroundings and thought I had passed to the other side. I found
myself standing with my back to a large lake, facing a great forest
of trees. There was no one in sight, and there was no boat upon
the lake or any other visible means to indicate how I might have
arrived there. I realized, or seemed to realize, that I had finished
my work in mortality and had gone home. I began to look around,
to see if I could not find someone. There was no evidence of anyone living there, just those great, beautiful trees in front of me
and the wonderful lake behind me.

I began to explore, and soon I found a trail through the woods
which seemed to have been used very little, and which was almost
obscured by grass. I followed this trail, and after I had walked
for some time and had traveled a considerable distance through
the forest, I saw a man coming towards me. I became aware that
he was a very large man, and I hurried my steps to reach him,
because I recognized him as my grandfather. In mortality he
weighed over three hundred pounds, so you may know he was a
large man. I remember how happy I was to see him coming. I had
been given his name and had always been proud of it.

When grandfather came within a few feet of me, he stopped.

His stopping was an invitation for me to stop. Then—and this I would like the boys and girls and young people never to forget—he looked at me very earnestly and said: "I would like to know what you have done with my name."

Everything I had ever done passed before me as though it were a flying picture on a screen—everything I had done. Quickly this vivid retrospect came down to the very time I was standing there. My whole life had passed before me. I smiled and looked at my grandfather and said: "I have never done anything with your name of which you need be ashamed."

He stepped forward and took me in his arms, and as he did so, I became conscious again of my earthly surroundings. My pillow was as wet as though water had been poured on it—wet with tears of gratitude that I could answer unashamed.

I have thought of this many times, and I want to tell you that I have been trying, more than ever since that time, to take care of that name. So I want to say to the boys and girls, to the young men and women, to the youth of the Church and of all the world: Honor your fathers and your mothers. Honor the names that you bear, because some day you will have the privilege and the obligation of reporting to them (and to your Father in heaven) what you have done with their name. (George Albert Smith, *Sharing the Gospel with Others* [Deseret Book Co., 1948], pp. 111-12.)

There were many during President Grant's administration who believed that he, being the seventh, would be the last president of the Church. The number seven had always played a significant role in ecclesiastical history, and this caused much comment in relation to the presidency of the Church.

But the Church not only sustained its eighth president in 1945 at his age of 73; it also found that he had an immediate important work to perform, which, because of his special abilities, he did exceptionally well. He was a man with a great heart of love, and his spirit and influence seemed important immediately after the conclusion of World War II. People's hearts were bleeding because of the loss of loved ones who had given their lives on each side of the great struggle for freedom and liberty. The faith of many was severely tested; they couldn't understand how a just and loving God could permit such things to happen as occurred during that terrible conflict. It is doubtful if during any previous war such terrible atrocities had occurred, at least to the same degree as the awful treatment accorded human beings at Dachau.

It was immediately following the conclusion of that war that President Smith, man of love—love of God, love of fellowmen, be they Mormon, or Jew, or Gentile, friend or enemy—became president of Christ's earthly church and kingdom.

The most critical need of the people of war-torn Europe was for fuel and for means to keep warm during the cold winter ahead. Fuel was needed for running trains and factories, for cooking and heating of homes. In many countries there were not even sufficient pots and pans, or stoves, since these had been confiscated by the Nazis to use in making munitions. Unless people could be clothed warmly, great suffering loomed in the months ahead.

People of the country and especially members of the Church were brought at that time to a realization that the now well-established Church welfare program was truly a revelation from God. During the war years the Relief Societies of the Church, directed by inspired leaders, had been making and storing quilts and blankets. With full realization of what the need would eventually be, each ward Relief Society had been asked to make and store at least 12 quilts and blankets over and above their own needs. Now the emergency had come, and all these quilts were called into the welfare program and many sent in 11-pound parcel post shipments to Saints abroad. Included in the packages sent were needles, thread, darning cottons, dehydrated soups, and other needed items. Canned goods were also available for shipping; sorely needed vitamins were being produced in the welfare program, and Churchwide clothing drives were being conducted.

It was on the occasion of a visit to Welfare Square in Salt Lake City to inspect the results of these clothing drives that President Smith demonstrated his true love for his neighbor. He made the visit with several of the welfare leaders, and the weather being somewhat cool, he was wearing a topcoat. As he stood before the open boxes where clothing was being gathered to be shipped to Europe, he removed his coat and laid it on one of the piles. Despite the protests of his associates, he insisted and returned to the Church offices without his coat.

The sending of these small packages of food, clothing, medicines, and such to Europe through the Red Cross and other agencies was felt by President Smith and his associates to be only scratching the surface. He took it upon himself to visit Washington, D.C., to find a solution to sending in carloads and shiploads the available stores of food, clothing, bedding, and other goods to needy sufferers of Europe.

With him were Elder John A. Widtsoe, Elder Thomas E. McKay, and myself. President Smith and his party called on President Harry S Truman and urged that ships be made available at once to carry welfare materials to the Latter-day Saints and others in the desolated countries of Europe.

President Truman listened sympathetically to President Smith's appeal and then inquired how long it would take to get together the items needed by the war victims. He was literally shocked and could not believe his own ears when President Smith said these items were available in large quantities for immediate shipment. President Truman then gave assurance of every possible help.

The party also called on members of President Truman's cabinet and the various ambassadors and representatives of nations in the interest of opening the doors for the receipt and distribution of the welfare items to the suffering people of Europe. Thus

The author pictured with President George Albert Smith at the start of one of many important journeys by railroad.

thousands of people were blessed by preparation that had been made under divine guidance, avoiding unnecessary delays in getting supplies to those in urgent need.

The following is quoted from the *Improvement Era* of December 1945, regarding this experience:

Little did the Prophet Joseph Smith realize when the Lord revealed to him the storehouse program for taking care of those in need that a hundred and fourteen years later it would mean the temporal salvation for his people in Europe. And little, too, did the members of the Church realize when the First Presidency announced in 1936 the organization of the Welfare program to assist the bishops and the branch presidents in the discharge of their duties . . . in searching after the poor to administer to their wants that their work on welfare projects in the production and storage of the necessities of life, would, in less than a decade, help to bring relief to a war-torn world.

President Smith always took occasion to give a religious message wherever he went and with whomever he met. He extended to President Truman best wishes for his success and assured him that the Latter-day Saints would pray constantly that God's blessing might attend him in his administration. Mr. Truman expressed his appreciation and said that he very much needed the faith and prayers of the people.

It was always President Smith's desire that the message of the restored gospel be shared with others. Besides his own missionary activities, he was always alert to tell the message of the gospel and to demonstrate by his life the love of the Master. President McKay said of him at his funeral services, "Our beloved leader has lived as nearly as it is humanly possible for a man to live a Christlike life."

President George Albert Smith said on more than one occasion the following:

Oh, how I wish that the good people of all organizations, all churches, might know what we are seeking to share with them. I meet members of the Catholics, the Presbyterians, the Methodists, the Baptists, and many other churches. I find in these

men and women virtues that are most beautiful to me. But, I find
that they are so rooted in the organizations with which they are
identified that when I try to explain to them what we are doing,
what we have in the Restored Gospel, they seem mystified; they
are not able to understand. One man said, "Would you have us
give up all that we have had, all these blessings that we have
enjoyed, to join your church?" I replied, "Not a blessing, not one
good thing would we ask you to give up. But, we do say to you, we
will be glad to share with you, if you will permit us to do so, without cost to you, some of the rich blessings of our Heavenly Father,
that you have not received and which are available to you now at
your very door."

Think what a marvelous opportunity we have. Think what a
great blessing it will be to us, if we do our part here, and then as
we stand on the other side of the Great Divide and our Father shall
summon his family together, as he will, to have these wonderful
men and women, hundreds of thousands of them who have been
our neighbors and who have watched our lives, stand there and
say, "Father in Heaven, we owe it to these thy children, of the
humble organization that bears the name of thy Son, that we understand the truth and that we are here at the supper of the Lamb."

That is our privilege and blessing.

It was the great humility and humanness of President Smith combined with his tremendous love for all
men that enabled him to accomplish an important and
not much heralded mission to Mexico in the first year
of his presidency. Its results were among the most
important of any in his ministry. Because of the very
nature of the mission, it had seemed wise that it be
undertaken by the president of the Church. It was the
first time in the history of the Church that a president
had visited the members in the Mexican Mission.

A rather large faction had broken away from the
Church in Mexico and established their own church.
They had the feeling that the Mexicans should take
charge of the branches and the mission in Mexico,
and they had other ideas that were not proper. They
were giving the Church a great deal of trouble. The
purpose of President Smith's visit was to encourage
these people to return to the Church and to welcome

them into church activity. Some hundreds of members had been out of harmony for the past ten years. His mission was successful and there was great rejoicing. (It was at that time that he dedicated the Ermita Ward chapel building in Mexico City, which was a very fine, commodious building.) These Mexican people participated in the services held by President Smith, who spoke in humility and sincerity. One of the leaders of the now reconciled group said, "There is only one president of The Church of Jesus Christ of Latter-day Saints, and he is here today."

While in Mexico City in 1945, President Smith; Arwell L. Pierce, president of the Mexican Mission; Harold Brown, who later became the first president of the Mexico City Stake; and I called on President Manuel Avilla Camacho of the Mexican Republic in the Government Palace. President Smith preached the gospel to President Camacho for about 20 minutes, and among other things told him about Joseph Smith's first vision, when he saw the Father and his Son, Jesus Christ.

President Smith on that occasion presented the Mexican president with a leather-bound copy of the Book of Mormon. The Mexican leader said, "My curiosity has been aroused considerably over that book; I would like to have one."

President Pierce said, "You are probably too busy to read it," and President Camacho answered, "No, I am going to read this."

President Smith also gave him the little book *A Short History of the Church* in English, and President Camacho inquired if we had a copy of that book in Spanish. President Pierce said, "No, but we are going to have it translated into Spanish."

In the course of the interview President Smith mentioned our recent visit with President Truman at the White House in Washington, and President

President George Albert Smith presents Book of Mormon to President Manuel Avilla Camacho of Mexico in 1946. With him are Joseph Anderson, Harold Brown, a missionary, Gustavo T. Serranno, Mexico's Secretary of Economics, and President Arwell L. Pierce of the Mexican Mission.

Camacho asked President Smith to send President Truman his greetings and his compliments on his success. Before we left Mexico President Smith wrote President Truman conveying to him as promised the greetings of the president of Mexico.

As we were leaving the palace following our interesting and historic visit, President Camacho said we might be assured that in him we had a friend in Mexico. He said that one of his government officials had been at our colonies in Chihuahua recently and had reported to him what we were doing there. He was aware that we had a fine school, the Juarez Academy, and were doing good work in agriculture. He shook hands with each of us as we left his reception room. President Smith asked the Lord to bless him and his people and expressed appreciation for the interview. President Camacho appeared to be greatly pleased.

As we entered the outer waiting room, we met Herbert Hoover, former president of the United States, who was waiting to keep an appointment with the Mexican president. We were pleased to shake hands with and greet Mr. Hoover, who asked that we remember him to President J. Reuben Clark, Jr., for whom he had real affection.

Though it is not generally known today, it was President Smith who took the lead in getting started the present-day work of the Church among the Lamanites. It was Elder Spencer W. Kimball of the Council of the Twelve, himself one of the foremost "servants" of the Indian people, who drew the attention of the Church to President Smith's part in initiating the missionary work among the Indians, when Elder Kimball said at the President's funeral services:

As his great love for his fellowmen began to grow into a great compassion, he saw in vision a certain whole people who went down from the proverbial Jerusalem to Jericho and they fell among thieves. He saw them stripped of their raiment and sorely wounded. He saw them deserted and deprived. He saw priests come by who saw their plight and passed by on the other side. He saw modern Levites who came and looked and passed by on the other side. President Smith determined it was time to do something constructive for these Indian people who had fallen into misfortune. He determined that it was time to bind up their wounds, and to pour thereon the oil.

He went to President Heber J. Grant [President Smith was then in the Council of the Twelve] and asked him for permission to do work among the Indian people, which was granted. A committee was organized and the work began in a small way as many programs do.

These words he said in one of his talks: "I have been intensely interested in doing something for the American Indians. I have traveled through several of the reservations; I have seen the need of something more being done for these children who are growing up. It remains for us who know and feel that these Indians, as we refer to them, are our Father's children.

"These Indians are descendants of a prophet of God who left Jerusalem 600 years before the birth of Christ. I have been in their homes, in many places, and have seen their poverty, their patience, and their forbearance." And then he went on and said: "I have had an interest in those Indians, and felt the urge to help, and only within the last two or three years have I had this opportunity and power to do something." He lived to see this work grow, from an infant organization, the Navajo-Zuni Mission, to the full fledged Southwest Indian Mission with more than a hundred missionaries.

Never before, in modern days at least, has there been in a conference or at a funeral such a large aggregation of Latter-day Saint Indians, and I know that if President Smith could see them here today his heart would go out to them in compassion, love, and appreciation.

About four years ago, President Smith made a visit to the Navajo Indian Reservation, taking Elder Cowley and myself with him. It was a missionary meeting, there being priests and ministers present from many of the sects and denominations. A hundred and fifty men and women were there. There were some disputations. Apparently some missionaries had gone to the hospital patients of other sects to bring relief and succor, and heated suggestions were made to restrict missionaries to visit only their own people.

President Smith in majesty stood up, and obtained the floor and said: "My friends, I am perplexed and shocked. I thought it would please me very much if any good Christian missionary of any denomination would be kind enough to visit me and bind up my wounds and pour on the sacred oil."

And then President Smith went on to tell them that this Church not only believes in tolerance, but also in understanding, and expressed the thought that long years ago Father Scanlan, a Roman Catholic Priest, conducted mass in the St. George Tabernacle at the suggestion and with permission of one of the Council of the Twelve and the president of the stake, who were there.

That happened on May 25, 1879. The priest had complained that he had no place in which he could conduct a mass for his people in southern Utah. The suggestion came from our brethren, and the mass was held. He had said, "We have no one to sing the Mass." The brethren had said, "You furnish the score; we will furnish the singers." And Catholic mass was conducted in a tabernacle.

He also told the group of ministers that the Church had also
assisted some of the Protestant denominations to get started in
Salt Lake City and in Utah.

There was general applause from these church dignitaries and
it was as though a magic word had been spoken, like the Master
spoke when he said "Peace, peace, be still." The waves of sus-
picion and antagonism became calm and placid.

I quoted as freely as I have from Elder Kimball
to firmly establish the interest, of which I was fully
aware, that President Smith had in the work of the
Church for the Indian and all other Lamanite people
including the Polynesians in the Pacific Islands,
whom he visited and for whom he demonstrated his
great love.

It was Elder Matthew Cowley, the first apostle
named to the Council of the Twelve by President
Smith after he became president of the Church, who
had recounted the great love of President Smith for
the Polynesians and the love they returned to him.
Said Elder Cowley:

On my first visit to Tonga . . . I called at the office of the
Prime Minister, Mr. Ata. The first thing he asked me was, "How
is my good friend, George Albert Smith? I have never met a
grander man in all my life than that man." When I called on the
crown prince, the Honorable Tungi, he brought from the drawer
of his desk an *Improvement Era* which he had just received from
President Smith.

At President Smith's funeral, Elder Cowley also
said:

In all the islands of the sea he is loved and revered, and on
his last visit to Hawaii during the centennial of that mission, in
his last testimony to those people, he said, "It is an honor to
have my name numbered among yours upon the membership records of The Church of Jesus Christ of Latter-day Saints."

So great was President Smith's capacity to love
and to help his fellowmen, especially the poor, the
discouraged, the underprivileged, the sick, that no one
ever knew or will ever know how often he went out of
his way to assist financially, to give comfort, cheer,

and encouragement. On his way home from the office
during his many years as a General Authority and
while he was president of the Church, he would go by
way of the home of a friend or someone who needed
the kind of comfort this humble, kindly, Christlike
man could give. He would never talk about these
visits, but somehow those who were the beneficiaries
would let it be known among their friends.

A special group in the Church and in the state of
Utah that had his constant help and interest were the
blind. Said one of these who knew of his interest and
service:

> Through the loving spirit of President George Albert Smith,
> the work for the blind in the Church has expanded, and reached
> out to touch the lives and enrich the lives of Latter-day Saint
> blind and gentiles. He believed in us and, because of that faith,
> we have learned to believe in ourselves and have been brought by
> a way we knew not.

It was at the funeral services for President Smith
that this same blind sister, Irene Jones, said, "Wednesday, April 4, 1951, was a dark day in the lives of
the blind, for we feel that we have lost one of the
dearest friends we will ever know, one of the greatest
humanitarians that ever lived. . . . He is not dead.
Such men forever live in the boundless measure of the
love they give."

Being a talented woman, Sister Jones had written
a special poem honoring President Smith at a reception given him on his seventieth birthday, 11 years
earlier. She had entitled it "An Understanding Heart,"
and at the request of the family, she read it at his
funeral services:

An Understanding Heart

When life beats hard with stormy hands
And bitter teardrops fall,
When friendless winter chills my soul
And empty echoes call,

'Tis then I turn with eager hope,
My steps though spent and lame,
To find an understanding heart
Where burns a friendly flame.
A heart where gentle wisdom dwells
Compassionate and kind;
Whose faith in God and man has taught
A like faith to the blind.

I lay my troubles at his feet,
Each trial, each bitter loss,
The burdens of a hundred more
He helps us bear the cross.
Consecrated by our Lord with apostolic light,
Consecreated in his soul,
He makes our darkness bright.
A loving radiance he sheds
That comes from God to man.
And we who walk in life-long night
Can see as others can.

Although his tender, loving face
From us is shut apart,
We see the gracious wisdom
Of his understanding heart.
We feel the peace within his soul
And know a peace our own;
We hear his silent prayer that tells:
We do not walk alone.
His faith in us will give us strength,
As unseen paths we plod,
Our souls uplifted by a man
In partnership with God.

I am aware as I review these pages that I have referred much to the funeral services for President Smith. This is not unusual, because those who spoke were his close associates in and out of the General Authorities of the Church and knew him as no others except perhaps his own immediate family. Most frequently spoken of was his great capacity to love—to love God, to love his fellowmen, and to love the gospel, which he desired to share with each of God's earthly children.

A selected few of these comments are yet needed to round out the word picture of this great, humble, approachable man, as I was privileged to know him.

Elder Cowley said:

He loved the people in the old 17th Ward, but he had so much love that he could not spend it all in that small area, and so God called him from the Seventeenth Ward and gave him to the world, and he went about the world among all nations giving his love and the love of God to his fellowmen. . . . His last message and instruction to me was, "Remember, young man, all the days of your life that you can find good in everyone if you will but look for it." . . . He loved everyone because he could see the good within them. He did not look upon sin with the least degree of allowance, but he loved the sinner because it is God's love that regenerates souls and may, by that process, transform the sinner into a saint. . . . Truly he forgave all men. He was aware in all of his life of the commandment of God: God will forgive whom he will forgive. As for us, we must forgive all men. He could do that, and then refer the matter to God. As he forgave I am sure he forgot.

Elder Kimball said:

Whenever I thought of our beloved President, I have always felt he was very, very near to the Kingdom of God. It seemed to me that every act, every thought of our President would indicate that with all of his heart and soul he loved the Lord, and loved his fellowmen. Is there a mortal being who could have loved them more? . . . The Lord Jesus Christ told us, "Be ye perfect, even as your Father which is in heaven is perfect." And so to compare President George Albert Smith with our Lord and Master I do not count a sacrilege, for perhaps he came nearer than the great majority of his contemporaries to that perfection. . . . The Savior said, "When ye come into a house, salute it, and if the house be worthy let your peace come upon it." And President Smith was much like that. There are homes from ocean to ocean and then from ocean to ocean again who have felt the peace that a great prophet has left in their homes.

On yet another occasion, President J. Reuben Clark, Jr., said of President Smith:

Throughout our association together, which has been close and intimate, and under various and trying circumstances, I have never known him even to indicate that he was impatient, that he had lost his temper, or even that he was under the necessity of controlling it. Evil slunk away from him at all times. It could not abide the presence of his righteous living. He was one of those few people of whom you can say he lived as he taught. I think that no man that we have had in the Church ever had a greater love for humanity than President George Albert Smith.

This is not intended to be a biography of this president of the Church with whom I was associated. I have endeavored through these pages to portray a man I learned to know and appreciate for the kind of leader he was and for the great love and compassion he had for me and for all of those about him. Without undue further detail, I should just call attention to the great service this man gave to the youth of the Church for many years in his capacity of general superintendent of the Young Men's Mutual Improvement Association. In his MIA leadership he also rose to some of the highest positions of prominence in the national and Church Boy Scout programs of any Church leader.

Though never robust in health, having been somewhat sickly as a youth and young man, President Smith drew on almost unbelievable reserves of physical strength as he performed the labors of his office for long hours, being constantly in the discharge of his duties of his high office without regard for his own welfare.

To accomplish all he did in his long lifetime, to develop the characteristics so aptly described in these preceding quoted comments, and to rise to the highest office in the Holy Priesthood of God upon the earth, President Smith lived strictly by a creed he adopted early in life. With a recital of this creed, which I can attest was truly and faithfully the pattern of his life, I close this chapter.

Creed of President George Albert Smith

I would be a friend to the friendless and find joy in ministering to the needs of the poor.

I would visit the sick and afflicted and inspire in them a desire for faith to be healed.

I would teach the truth to the understanding and blessing of all mankind.

I would seek out the erring one and try to win him back to a righteous and happy life.

I would not seek to force people to live up to my ideals, but rather love them into doing the thing that is right.

I would live with the masses and help to solve their problems, that their earth life may be happy.

I would avoid the publicity of high positions and discourage the flattery of thoughtless friends.

I would not knowingly wound the feeling of any, not even one who may have wronged me, but would seek to do him good and make him my friend.

I would overcome the tendency to selfishness and jealousy and rejoice in the success of all the children of my Heavenly Father.

I would not be an enemy to any living soul.

Knowing that the Redeemer of mankind has offered to the world the only plan that will fully develop us and make us really happy here and hereafter, I feel it not only a duty but a blessed privilege to disseminate this truth.

SECTION THREE

Leadership of President David O. McKay

5

President McKay, A Man of Worldwide Vision

I have often said that I have had two great teachers in my life—my own mother and President David O. McKay. I think that my acquaintance with President McKay dated as far back as, if not farther than, that of any of the living General Authorities. I knew him from the time I was a boy of 14 when I attended the Weber Academy in Ogden.

I was just a country boy living in Roy, Utah, when I attended the Weber Academy and during most of the school season rode horseback to Ogden. My folks were not successful farmers and were very limited in means. It was not possible for them to assist me, to any great extent at least, in meeting the expenses of an education. Accordingly I worked at the canning factory in Roy each year while attending the academy to get sufficient money to pay tuition and other expenses. Therefore, I was about six weeks late each year in enrolling in the school.

David O. McKay was at that time a young man in his early thirties, and yet was principal of the academy. He was also the English teacher. He was then, as he remained during his entire life, a tall, handsome man with an outstanding personality, and

was easily the greatest schoolteacher I remember.
The lessons I learned in his English classes remained
with me all my life.

When President David O. McKay, left, became president in 1951, he
selected Stephen L Richards, center, and J. Reuben Clark Jr. right, as
his counselors.

Being a country boy, naturally bashful and backward, and always a few weeks late in starting, I had a
difficult time in the classes to begin with. I shall never
forget my embarrassment when this great teacher-
principal would call me to the blackboard to demonstrate before the class the diagraming of sentences.
He also won the love and admiration of the students
by the way he taught us some of the English classics.
He taught them in such a way that showed his great
love for them and made them so come to life for us

that few of us ever forgot them. I shall never forget the beauty of such literature as "The Lady of the Lake" and "The Princess," as taught to us by him.

He made the classes in such literature so interesting that they were never dull. In fact, he became so interested in his subject that he frequently failed to hear the bell that indicated the hour was up.

On various occasions in later years, President McKay and I discussed at some length our relationship in the schoolroom many years previously. He remembered very well the time when I was one of his students. On one occasion when he was in the hospital two or three years before he passed away, we were discussing the past, and I reminded him of the influence his teaching had had upon me and repeated to him some of the verses of "The Lady of the Lake," which I still remember, and reviewed with him the manner in which he had taught us to repeat these verses. He seemed very pleased, as any teacher might be, to know that the things he taught so many years previously were still fresh in the mind of his student.

As a matter of fact, President McKay was my teacher most of my life. He was one of the Council of the Twelve when I started working for President Grant. When my duties first required that I attend the weekly meetings of the First Presidency and the Twelve in the Salt Lake Temple, he was one of this circle of great men. He later became a counselor in the First Presidency and subsequently president of the Church. With each of these moves my association with him became closer and more intimate, and I have often thought that seldom did I have the privilege of association with him in any capacity that I did not learn something from him either by precept or by example.

I often recall the intensely piercing eyes of President McKay and how, as he was interviewing me or discussing matters of importance, they seemed to be looking right into my soul. He never dropped his gaze, and it seemed as if my very mind and thoughts were being laid bare before him.

I think that I seldom, if ever, called on President McKay in his office or in his home or apartment in the Hotel Utah—and such contacts were numberless—that I did not learn something from him. He was a man who had great control over himself. I have seen him under extreme pressures when under such conditions he could easily have lost his temper, but I never knew him to say an angry word. He may have felt annoyance, and rightly did on certain occasions, but he had great control over his speech, his language, and his attitude.

President McKay was always a remarkable specimen of physical manhood. From the very earliest days I knew him, long before his hair had begun to turn white, he wielded a remarkable influence among his fellowmen. Throughout his life his inspiring personality, sense of humor, and sparkling demeanor won many friends for himself and for the Church.

As president of the Church, David O. McKay stood out as a remarkable leader and as a prophet and teacher of his people. He was never afraid to make decisions when he felt those decisions were inspired of the Lord. Often as I listened to discussions he had with his counselors and with the Council of the Twelve, I heard him give his decision after first saying, "I feel impressed." There was never a time when decisions were rendered by him in such a manner that I was not certain that this great prophet had sought the inspiration to which he was entitled and the Spirit of the Lord had dictated the answer.

President McKay was a man of action. Whenever a question was before him, he did not hesitate to act regarding it if he was satisfied that it was his responsibility and duty to act and when he felt that the inspiration of the Lord was directing him. I have never known a man who was more inclined to make decisions on matters requiring decision. He was a true prophet of the Lord, and many was the time, of a weighty discussion, in the course of which I heard him make a pronouncement that seemed like a revelation direct from the Lord and which, as a matter of fact, was the word of the Lord through his prophet. When the statement was made, in the manner indicated, those present had no further argument regarding the matter. They recognized that the Lord had spoken.

President McKay recognized that he was entitled to the inspiration and revelation of the Lord, and during his administration he accomplished great things as the Lord's earthly representative. The Church made wonderful progress during the 20 years of his leadership. It was during these years that the Church grew to become recognized as a worldwide organization, with the full blessings of the restored gospel being made available to members of the Church in many parts of the world. It was his worldwide vision that directed that temples be built abroad for easier access by the Saints and that stakes be created in foreign lands to strengthen the organizations and activities of the members. Now in many lands and in many languages the blessings of temple endowments, sealings, and marriages for the living and the dead are performed. The first stakes in Europe and in other parts of the world, such as Australia, New Zealand, and South America, were organized during his presidency. This set a pattern for the Church, and now almost monthly a new foreign-language stake is organized, presided over by natives of the various countries and island empires, giving evidence that Zion is being strengthened in her stakes on a worldwide basis.

Perhaps the foundation for this worldwide vision

President McKay developed in relation to the Church was laid years before he became president. In 1921, as a young and vigorous apostle, he undertook, by direction of President Grant and his counselors, the first worldwide tour of all the missions of the Church by a General Authority. With his companion, Hugh J. Cannon, he spent the whole of the year visiting the far-flung missions, getting acquainted with the people of many nations, meeting the Saints and gaining first-hand knowledge of their lands, customs, and traditions, and finding assurance of their great faith and devotion to the Church. The published accounts of this world mission tour reveal many faith-promoting and spiritual experiences that could only come to one who lived close to the Lord and was guided and prompted by the Holy Spirit. These accounts of speaking in tongues, being directed among strange people in strange lands, and being saved from harm and even impending death, give us to know that the age of miracles is far from past in the kingdom of God today.

President McKay should always be remembered as one under whose leadership were built meetinghouses, temples, schools, and other Church buildings throughout the world. But who can possibly deny that his predecessors should have their share of recognition for helping to prepare the way. As have all the presidents of the Church, President McKay built well on the solid foundations laid by the prophets who preceded him.

The presidents I have known have all been great friend-makers for the Church. When President McKay dedicated the temple in London, he declared that a new era had commenced. How prophetic and true that has been! There has since been a great upsurge of missionary converts, and the spirit of missionary work has grown tremendously. It is marvelous how the Lord is pouring out his Spirit upon the people. The time is short, and the little stone that was cut out of the mountain without hands is rolling forth and filling the earth.

As I look back, I feel gratitude for the experience that was mine in partaking of President McKay's judgment, inspiration, and leadership abilities. It was an inspiration to come under the influence of his genial personality, to witness his kindly attitude toward the unfortunate, and to recognize the wisdom and inspiration of his decisions.

As an evidence of the great personal radiation that emanated from him, I quote from an article in the *Instructor* (March 1956) written by Elder Harold B. Lee:

President McKay is one of the greatest teachers—and I use that word *great* without any hesitancy. I wish every teacher could realize what power he may wield upon all with whom he comes in contact even as President McKay makes an impression upon all who come into his presence. Some years ago a feature writer came here to write a magazine story for a national publication. President McKay was kind enough to give him a little time. After two or three hours, President McKay called and asked if I would take this man to Welfare Square.

On the way there this man said to me, "I've had today the most unusual experience of my life."

He said, "My editors assigned me to write a story, and of course it's always written around some personality. They flew me up from South America here. I'll fly back east and go to Europe and Asia. And always I'm meeting personalities—the great personalities of every country. But this morning I have met a man who has made a greater impression upon me than any other man I have ever met."

He continued, "You know, as President McKay sat across his desk and looked at me with those great eyes, he actually made me feel as if I wanted to be a better man. I actually thought I ought to quit smoking after I'd been in President McKay's company."

Such a thing could be that one might have felt in his heart some sense of resentment against President McKay because of an imagined injury, but when he looked at you with those wonderful, impressive eyes, and that heartwarming smile came across his face, one could only have a feeling of love for him. Any feeling of resentment would disappear like snow before a summer sun.

Man is without doubt God's greatest creation. Like his predecessors and those who have succeeded him as presidents of the Church, President McKay was born great. He no doubt inherited a remarkable degree of greatness from his ancestors, but one's personality is what one makes of it. He developed a magnetic personality by living a clean, exemplary life, a life of unselfish service, and by devoting himself to those virtues which make for character and personality. To influence others for good is to grow. The influence of these divinely inspired prophets throughout the Church, wherever their services have taken them, has brought increased righteousness to all who have been touched by their influence.

President McKay understood fully and exemplified in his life the true spirit of gratitude. He was graciously appreciative of everything that was done for him. During most of the nearly 20 years he presided over the Church, on the occasion of his birthdays the employees of the First Presidency's office gathered together to wish him a happy birthday, enjoy some light refreshments, and give him a small gift. On one of these occasions we gave him a pair of shoes, and he in return gave us a great lesson on the meaning of gratitude. He said:

Brother Murdock, Brother Herrick, brothers and sisters all, these occasions and others that you have held similar to this one make one realize the difference between thanks and gratitude. Thank you is of lips, the tone of the voice; gratitude is from the heart, and it is with gratitude that I accept your tribute. It does not seem much probably. The occasion is a simple one, a birthday greeting, but you know these incidents—occasions—go on forever. I was reminded just the other day of that fact. I reached into my library—I was studying for another purpose—and I turned to a volume of favorite poems, and I thought, "That was given to me in school, in the Weber Academy," so before I looked for a poem I turned to the inscription. There were twenty-four names of students in the Weber Academy 49 years ago, 1908, nearly half a century. I read their names. Gray-haired women now, those living, and some on the other side. Well, what memories crowded my mind that hour in the library. I thought of the time when they came as a class and presented that book of favorite poems. How quickly, swiftly the years in that half century have passed, but the very feelings of gratitude that I had when those young girls came and presented that little present were reawakened in my heart.

And so it is with your gifts during these last few years and today. It will not be just the memory of wearing shoes, but your names that I had last year and that I want this year will be filed with my memories, and I wish that fifty years from now I could still read them. That may not be here, but the affection accompanying this gift, the affection with which I receive it will last through eternity. That is what I mean by gratitude coming from the heart. It is easily spoken, but these messages given in concert as you have given today remain in the heart and memory forever.

Thank you and God bless you.

On another occasion, a thank-you letter addressed to me contained not only a typical expression of his appreciation but a bit of his philosophy about growing old. It read:

September 15, 1961

Dear Brother Anderson:

I want to again thank you for your participating in presenting to me that beautiful automatic Swiss watch. I shall never forget the friendly spirit and feeling of brotherhood that existed at that gathering of the employees in the office of the First Presidency on the eve of my eighty-eighth birthday. I shall always cherish the memory of that occasion!

For the past several years, I have been prone to consider old age as a disagreeable, unwelcome trespasser, skulking along to claim any faculty that might show the strain and usage of the passing years; this year at eighty-eight, I look upon him with a degree of compassion akin to appreciation. Indeed if it were not for "Old Age" I should not have been seventy-five, or eighty, or eighty-five, and most assuredly not eighty-eight.

Now I am content to let him walk by my side, but shall continue as long as possible to deny the demands of old age to take from me the good health Kind Providence still gives me.

Sister McKay, thankfully regaining her strength and activity, joins me in this expression of appreciation.

Cordially and sincerely,
David O. McKay.

My imtimate acquaintance and association with President McKay during the last few years of his life, when he was not in good health physically, was an especially interesting and profitable experience. Notwithstanding the weakness of his legs and other physical infirmities, his mind was clear, and the Lord inspired him in the decisions he made and in his direction of the weighty affairs of the Church. The scepter of his leadership did not fall from him, and the Lord sustained him constantly. The problems he was required to wrestle with were heavy indeed, but the Lord sustained him fully in his leadership until the last few weeks.

His remarkable sense of humor never left him, and I will never forget his courageous attitude. He was always very much the gentleman, and his love for the Brethren, his associates, was always as deep and complete as one man can have for another. His was to the very end a great example of the love which can only be found in those who are witnesses of the Lord Jesus Christ and devoted to the great cause of the gospel kingdom.

I have always felt that I was on sacred ground when I attended the meetings of the General Authorities in the temple and heard them in humility bear testimony of their love for the work and for one another. I knew their utterances came from the heart. The Spirit of the Lord is always there in rich measure, and those who participate and listen get a true understanding of the spirit of brotherhood and an insight into the thinking that emanates from these men, the purity of their hearts, and the inspiration that guides them.

I relate an experience that shows the great ties of brotherhood and spirituality that bind these Brethren together. It is an excerpt from a talk given by President McKay at the California missionary conference on Saturday afternoon, January 3, 1952. I present it here for two reasons: one, it is a remarkable experience through which President McKay passed that could have prevented his subsequently becoming president of the Church; and two, it is a remarkable evidence of the power of the priesthood as exercised by President Grant in his prophetic blessing. President McKay told the missionaries:

In March, 1916, the Ogden River was a turbulent stream. The road was washed out. My brother, Thomas E., was marooned in Ogden. He was living up in Huntsville, and Wednesday evening he came to our house, picked up the telephone, and telephoned his wife, saying, "Will you please send a horse down with the road supervisor to where they are repairing the road and I will come home."

As he hung up the telephone, he said to my young son, Lawrence: "Will you drive me up tomorrow morning to the canyon, and I will ride the horse from there home?" That afternoon I had taken the children up to see the torrent, and I said, "No, I will drive you, Tommy, if you get up early enough."

Next morning, Thursday morning, when I should have been in Salt Lake to attend Council meeting, for the first time that winter the furnace was out, and I was delayed in starting the furnace. When I came up into the kitchen, the clock pointed to quarter to seven o'clock. That was just the time that I usually got ready to catch the Bamberger train at seven forty-five, and I thought, 'I can't go.'

Something said: "Go up to the bridge and back." I said, "Come on, Tommy [Thomas E. McKay], I'll take you up." It was pouring, but the little Ford splashed up 21st Street there, better than it ever ran before. Going up there Thomas E., not knowing anything about that impression, said, "I think you had better not attempt to cross the bridge."

The day before I had seen rocks piled there to keep the bridge from washing out at the mouth of the canyon. But we were there at that bridge so quickly—it seemed less than five minutes—for we drove at a speed through muck and mud and rain, and neglecting the inspiration, or whatever you may call it, and using my experience of yesterday, I said, "I believe I will cross the bridge. Can you swim if the bridge gives way?"

Before he could answer we had crossed the bridge, and I heard him say: "Look out, there's a rope!" Stretched across the road was one of these large derrick ropes. Before I could reach for the emergency brake, we hit the rope which broke the windshield; it came back and struck me, severing my lip and cheek, catching my upper lip, breaking my jaw, and I was unconscious. Thomas E. ducked and was unhurt. I knew no more until we were back in Ogden. Returning, I heard him say, "I think I will take you to the hospital." I looked, and there in my hand were extracted teeth and blood, and I said: "No, take me home."

I will not take time tonight to tell you the whole story. That was Thursday morning. It was not long before I was on the operating table and when I came to in the room, the nurse, to comfort me, said, "Well, you can wear a beard." That I would be disfigured for life was taken for granted. They had taken thirteen stitches putting the jaw back, sewing up the side of the lip and cheek, and my face, of course, was swollen beyond recognition.

In testimony of that I will give the words of Peter G. Johnston, my first missionary companion in Scotland, who, having heard over the radio of the accident, came down from Idaho, an act of friendship which I shall never never forget. The door happened to be open that morning—this was the morning after—and as he passed the room, he did not recognize the man lying there on the bed, but he came back, and the nurse said, "Yes, that is he." He stood at the bed and looked. "Well," he said, smiling as best he could, "the eyes are the same anyhow."

Bishop Olson, Heber Scowcroft, and President Thomas B. Evans were there at my side soon after the operation, and administered to me, and Bishop Olson, my own bishop, said in that prayer: "We bless you that you shall not have pain."

Next day President Heber J. Grant, who was the President of the Twelve then, came, and he said, "David, you are not to talk, but I will give you a blessing." And in his blessing he said, "I bless you that you shall not be disfigured, and that you shall not be scarred."

Later, at a reunion given by President Nibley at the Hotel Utah, President Grant looked at me from a distance, and he said,

"David, I do not see any scars, but when I took my hands off your head, I wondered about what I had said, whether I had made a mistake."

One of his great statements, for which President McKay will long be remembered, is "No other success can compensate for failure in the home." In his home and family life he was exemplary. Though he had great love for his fellowmen, he had greater affection for his lovely companion and his children. To them, he was always the exemplary husband and father, and as President McKay and Sister McKay grew older, their great love for each other and the example of their lives in living the principles of the gospel became legendary throughout the Church. To his sweetheart he was always loving, considerate, and courteous. He was by nature courteous. I have never been with him in his office or home but that he arose to his feet when Sister McKay entered the room. This courteous regard for his sweetheart and companion was so inborn into his nature that when he became physically unable to arise, he was observed at least to make the effort instinctively.

On one occasion—it was their sixty-ninth wedding anniversary and just two or three weeks before President McKay passed away—President Alvin R. Dyer and I visited them in their apartment in the Hotel Utah. Neither of them was well at the time, but they were well groomed, as they always were, and sitting on a couch in the living room holding hands. This too was a McKay tradition. On frequent occasions they were to be seen holding hands.

In the course of our conversation I asked Sister McKay how she was, and she said, "I am all right, but I am concerned about my boy." I said, "He is still your boy, is he?" She answered quickly, "He surely is." To this I said, "He is the best, is he not?" and she answered, "Most certainly."

President McKay would never go to a temple meeting or elsewhere from her presence without kissing her goodbye. When I think of the fact that my acquaintance with both of them went back to the time when they were young and energetic, without physical or other handicaps, and that that acquaintance persisted over those many years, I must express gratitude to the Lord for my acquaintance with such wonderful people and for the lessons I learned from President McKay.

This great man's sermons over the years would fill many volumes. They have appeared in the *Conference Reports* and Church magazines and periodicals. He was the most widely traveled president of the Church, his journeys estimated to have covered over two million miles. His talks were at conferences, temple and other building dedications, funerals, patriotic meetings, and other important occasions too numerous to mention.

Most of his messages were filled with poetic quotations from the world's best literature and illustrations from life that serve as windows through which the light of understanding is shown, to enlighten the souls of men with the truths of the eternal gospel. Most of the poems he quoted from memory, for he never forgot the lovely literary gems learned in earlier life when he was a student and teacher. His sermons contained doctrinal and ethical discussions and instructions to the Latter-day Saints and to our Father's children generally. They are inspired classics that will never become outmoded. Many of his sermons and life's experiences will be and have been published.

I have made a selection of some of his statements, which are not intended in any way to be complete, but merely as an indication of the nature of his thinking as expressed on various occasions and to reveal the greatness of his philosophy of life, his love of mankind, and his awareness of the world about him.

Here are some of the statements I have chosen:

Man's chief concern in life should not be the acquiring of gold, or of fame. or of material possessions. It should not be development of physical powers, nor of intellectual strength, but his aim, the highest in life, should be the development of a Christ-like character.

*** ***

The finest thing for young people and everybody is to live the gospel.

*** ***

Young people do not seem to realize that the religious life is the happy life. Doing for others, making others happy, and living the gospel of Jesus Christ is the really happy life for everybody to live.

*** ***

The real tragedy in America is not that we have permitted the Bible to slip out of our schools, but that we have so openly neglected to teach it in either the home or the Church.

*** ***

Never before was there such need of revitalizing the teaching of faith and repentance on the part of parents. Never before in the history of our country was the State in greater need of young men and young women who cherish the higher life in preference to the sordid, the selfish, and the obscene.

*** ***

Teach the boys that it is chastity during youth that gives vigor, strength, and virility of manhood. Teach the girls that chastity is the crown of beautiful womanhood.

*** ***

A spotless character, founded upon the ability to say "no" in the presence of those who mock and jeer wins the respect and love of men and women whose opinion is most worthwhile. Drinking and petting parties form an environment in which the moral sense becomes dulled and unbridled passion holds sway. It then becomes easy to take the final step downward in moral disgrace.

*** ***

Ten Rules of Happiness

1. Develop yourself by self-discipline.
2. Joy comes through creation—sorrow through destruction.

Every living thing can grow; use the world wisely to realize soul growth.

3. Do things which are hard to do.

4. Entertain upbuilding thoughts. What you think about when you do not have to think shows what you really are.

5. Do your best this hour, and you will do better the next.

6. Be true to those who trust you.

7. Pray for wisdom, courage, and a kind heart.

8. Give heed to God's messages through inspiration. If self-indulgence, jealousy, avarice, or worry have deadened your response, pray to the Lord to wipe out these impediments.

9. True friends enrich life. If you would have friends, be one.

10. Faith is the foundation of all things—including happiness.

The following responses are some that came from young people to the news of the death of President David O. McKay in answer to the question. What influence did President McKay have on your life?

"He just glowed with love."

"He was like a partner in our home at all times."

"He never chastised anyone—he just put his arm of love around the world."

"When President McKay died, we felt that we had lost someone in our own family."

"We have lost a personal friend."

"If only the young people of today will remember his teachings."

The following is a list of answers that were given to the question, "What teachings of President McKay do you remember best?"

"Love thy mother and father all the days of your lives."

"Be clean in mind and body, always."

"Smile."

"Be reverent every day, not just on Sunday."

"Pray together."

"Read good books."

"Study the scriptures."

"Hate no one."

"Be pleasant and courteous to everyone."

"Dress modestly—our Father in heaven is watching."

"Marriage: the temple way is the only way."

I shall always remember some of his thoughts expressed at the dedication of the Oakland Temple in 1964. In nearly all of his remarks, President McKay mentioned that there were spirits from the other world who were present. And he mentioned too that there are, in the air, waves passing back and forth all the time, but we do not respond to them. He explained that there is the sweet voice of a singer on the other side of the world, but we do not hear it. There are the phrases of a great orator over in one of the other countries passing through the air, but we are dead to those things. However, if we turn on the radio and get in tune and harmony with those infinite moving waves, we hear the singing, we hear the phrases and the tones just as clearly as if we were in their presence. That, he said, is true of the impressions that come to man, through the Holy Ghost, and if we were in tune with the spirit world, we could hear the voices of our loved ones.

Suffice it to say in closing this chapter that the ninth President of the Church, David O. McKay, faithfully accomplished the work that the Lord assigned to him before he left the preexistent world to take upon himself mortality. He served as the mouthpiece of the Lord in the period allotted to him in the dispensation of the fulness of times. .

6

Counselors to President McKay

When President David O. McKay's career as a General Authority ended in January 1970, he had established several records for longevity of service. He had lived to a greater age than any previous General Authority, death coming to him about four months past his ninety-sixth birthday. He had also been a General Authority longer than any other in this dispensation, a total of 63 years and eight months. Only one other had exceeded the total of 35 years as a member of the First Presidency accumulated by President McKay, and that was President Joseph F. Smith, whose total was 38 years.

When President McKay became president of the Church in April 1951, he had completed more than 16 years as second counselor in the First Presidency, serving with both President Heber J. Grant and President George Albert Smith. During these same years President J. Reuben Clark Jr., had served as first counselor in the First Presidency.

At the Solemn Assembly in the Salt Lake Tabernacle on April 9, 1951, President McKay announced to the Church his choice of counselors—President Stephen L Richards as first counselor and President Clark as second counselor. He made the explanation to the

Following the death of President Richards and later, President Clark, others who served as counselors to President McKay were Henry D. Moyle, Hugh B. Brown, and Nathan Eldon Tanner.

Church that the reason for sustaining his counselors in
that order was based on their seniority in the Council
of the Twelve. It was on that occasion also that President Clark made his now historic statement that it
mattered not where but how one served in the kingdom
of God, and he pledged his full loyalty and support to
President McKay and President Richards.

Thus the counselors to President McKay during
the nearly 20 years of his service as president of the
Church were:

> Stephen L. Richards—first counselor, April 1951 to
> May 1959

> J. Reuben Clark, Jr.—second counselor, April 1951
> to June 1959
> —first counselor, June 1959 to October 1961

> Henry D. Moyle—second counselor, June 1959 to
> October 1961
> —first counselor, October 1961 to September 1963

> Hugh B. Brown—second counselor, October 1961
> to October 1963
> —first counselor, October 1963 to January 1970

> Nathan Eldon Tanner—second counselor, October
> 1963 to January 1970

Since I have previously given an extensive account
of my long service with President Clark, he will not be
further introduced in this chapter, but I will endeavor
to introduce the others named above, for I have had
a close, intimate association with each of them and
sincerely acknowledge their devotion and loyal dedication to their illustrious file leader.

During his presidency, President McKay called
others into service as counselors in the First Presidency.
President Brown had such a position from June 1961
until October of that same year when he became second

counselor. Two others were called as counselors in the First Presidency on the same day, October 28, 1965. They were Joseph Fielding Smith, then President of the Council of the Twelve, who continued in that position, and Elder Thorpe B. Isaacson, then an Assistant to the Twelve. Elder Alvin R. Dyer, also an Assistant to the Twelve, was called by President McKay as a counselor in the First Presidency, in April 1968. He had previously been ordained an apostle by President McKay on October 5, 1967.

Following President McKay's death and the reorganization of the First Presidency in January 1970, President Hugh B. Brown was returned to his position of seniority in the Council of the Twelve, and Elders Isaacson and Dyer again resumed their places among the Assistants to the Twelve.

I feel impressed to add at this point that with each new change in the First Presidency I have witnessed during these many years, I have marveled at the blending of the wills of strong and capable men of varied experiences and achievements into a unity of purpose— the building of the kingdom of God on earth. It is further evidence of the divinity of the restored gospel of Jesus Christ.

PRESIDENT STEPHEN L RICHARDS

When Stephen L Richards became a counselor in the First Presidency, he rose to a position once held by his illustrious grandfather, Willard Richards, who was an associate of Joseph Smith and a fellow prisoner in Carthage Jail at the time of the martyrdom. Willard Richards remained true and faithful to the memory of the first Prophet of this dispensation and was among the stalwart pioneer leaders, later becoming a counselor to Brigham Young when the First Presidency was reestablished in December 1847.

President Stephen L Richards had already had the honor of following in his grandfather's footsteps in his ordination as an apostle and member of the Council of the Twelve. In this respect he was one of a large number of descendants of early stalwart associates of the Prophet Joseph Smith who, in second, third, or fourth generations, honored the names of their forebears by rising to positions of prominence in Church leadership. A few of them with whom I have had the privilege of associating these past 50 years include President Grant, George Albert Smith, George F. Richards, Joseph Fielding Smith, Joseph F. Merrill, Sylvester Q. Cannon, Spencer W. Kimball, Ezra Taft Benson, and LeGrand Richards.

Stephen L Richards attracted my admiration from the time I first met him in the Council of the Twelve meetings in the temple. I soon learned to watch his reaction to questions under discussion and discovered that not only was his opinion sound, given after thorough, analytical thinking, but that the recommendations that he frequently made after summing up the discussions very often became the sentiment of the group and the action of the Council.

I found that this man had the happy faculty of being able to analyze a problem thoroughly, seemingly not overlooking any possible contingency. He had an astute, analytical mind, great wisdom and capacity, and his judgment was dependable. Perhaps he had attained these skills by a native intelligence highly trained in the legal profession. During his professional life before being named to the Council of the Twelve in 1917, he had been a successful practicing attorney and member of the University of Utah Law School faculty.

As both an apostle and a member of the First Presidency, President Richards was not easily swayed from a decision once he had reached a conclusion that his analysis of the problem at hand was right. This I found, however, did not deter him from deferring to the decisions and feelings of the prophets he served, because of his great faith that the Lord's inspiration was manifest through them. He was forthright and fearless in expressing his feelings, usually in a voice of quiet persuasion and thorough consideration of the opinions expressed by others.

The sermons of President Richards, in my estimation, portrayed deep and profound thinking and were literary classics in their construction and composition. While in his later years his talks were generally written beforehand and read by him on the occasion of their delivery, yet, when in earlier years he spoke without the written manuscript before him, his language was practically word perfect when spoken. His corrections on the shorthand reporter's copy were very few indeed.

President Richards was a deep thinker and scholar. One need only read his many sermons to appreciate the truth of this statement. While his demeanor toward the employees and clerical staff seemed somewhat reserved, yet few, if any, have been so generous and kind in their commendation of my reports of council meetings as was President Richards. Such commendation naturally was greatly appreciated as I attempted to make proper and complete, yet concise, minutes and notes of discussions and actions upon which are based the conduct and history of the divine church of our Redeemer. Particularly has this been the case when among those assembled in these councils were men such as President Grant, President McKay, President Joseph Fielding Smith, President Richards, President Clark, James E. Talmage, Orson F. Whitney, and President Harold B. Lee, to name only a few of the outstanding ones during my many years of service.

My experiences and travels have brought me into contact with many of those whom we look upon as the great men of the world in business, finance, industry, and politics. I have been highly and favorably impressed by their judgment, wisdom, ability, and courtesy. There have been among them many of the great and noble men of the earth, honorable and good men, and they have played and are playing important roles in their particular fields, but enduring peace can never come to the world nor can men find true happiness until they accept and abide by the teachings of our Lord and Master. Nowhere can they find these teachings better exemplified than in the lives of true, faithful, devoted Latter-day Saints, such as the life of Stephen L Richards.

He always had a strong conviction that a man's contributions to society were all important and that they were by no means always determined by educational achievements. I have always remembered for the lesson it taught me and others the speech he gave at a Brigham Young University devotional in February 1957. His message and illustration used in these excerpts were the true sentiments of this profound thinker:

I suppose that there may be a large proportion of our student-body who have already determined upon their vocations, and that they are working to the end of qualifying themselves to carry forward a legitimate vocation in life, and there may be others who are awaiting the determination until after they shall have had the education, and after they have appraised the opportunities which are available. Of course, the choice of a vocation is an individual matter. I have no doubt in this modern day that you take advantage of some of these estimates that are made of aptitude—I suppose they are helpful—to determine whether you are best fitted for a lawyer, an engineer, a teacher, or some other vocation.

It doesn't take, necessarily, one of these high-sounding, so-called aristocratic professions to give a person the opportunity to do a great service in the world. I have great respect for a professional life and professional contribution, but I have likewise a very great respect for the so-called humbler vocations which in themselves make high contributions to our society. No matter how humble, if the job is well done, it will be of value, and it will be of value to the people. To help others is, after all, the end of our service.

Two things are essential for success in any vocation, I would say: *character* and *ability*. I have seen people with one without the other, and I have seen some moderate success come. But I wouldn't hire anybody with the utmost ability without some character, and of course I wouldn't want to hire anybody without the ability to help me. Character and ability—and I believe we can secure that character and that ability by the inculcation of the ideals that the Church of our Lord holds out to us.

Speaking of the humble calling—maybe I have told you this story before—but years ago, when the pioneers were coming west, there was maintained at the office of the President of the Church a big book called the "Register." Every immigrant was expected to go to that office, sign his name, and put oppostite his name his vocation or his trade. They wanted to know who were blacksmiths, who were carpenters, etc. Well, there came a man who went to the offices of the President, and he signed his name "William Fowler, laborer." He had no trade. But in the heart of that man was a great sentiment which, as you will recognize, found expression in that marvelous hymn, the most popular among our people for now nearly a century of time. That sentiment in that humble man's heart performed for the Church a service the like of which few have ever performed:

> We thank thee, O God, for a prophet
> To guide us in these latter days.
> We thank thee for sending the gospel
> To lighten our minds with its rays.
> We thank thee for every blessing
> Bestowed by thy bounteous hand.
> We feel it a pleasure to serve thee,
> And love to obey thy command.

One of the most important features of that verse is, "We love to obey thy command." Well, that sentiment so endeared that man to the heart of the Church that, when he died, the Church caused a monument to be placed above his grave down in Manti. . . . On the monument are inscribed these simple words: "To the memory of William Fowler, author of the hymn, We Thank Thee, O God, for a Prophet."

So, one doesn't need a great vocation to offer the opportunities for wonderful service.

It was no surprise to any of President McKay's associates when the newly sustained president of the Church named Stephen L Richards as a counselor. Theirs had often been referred to as a "Damon and Pythias relationship," for they were true personal friends, confidants as well as associates, among the General Authorities.

Sunday School leadership was no small part of the life of President McKay, and at his side for most of these years of leadership in this worldwide gospel teaching auxiliary of the Church was Stephen L. Richards. President Richards had had considerable Sunday School experience. His first official position was as a secretary and teacher in the Sugar House Ward Sunday School. Among other positions were those of assistant stake superintendent in the Salt Lake Stake and later a member of the Granite Stake Sunday School board. In 1906 he was named to the general Sunday School board. This was the same year that President McKay was called to the apostleship and named as second assistant general superintendent of the Sunday Schools.

In April 1909, President McKay was advanced to first assistant superintendent and was succeeded as second assistant superintendent by Stephen L Richards.

Thus began a close association and friendship that ripened with the years. In November 1918 Elder McKay, then an apostle, was named general Sunday School superintendent, and his assistants were Stephen L Richards, also an apostle, and George D. Pyper. In the meantime, in January 1917, Elder McKay was privileged to welcome his beloved friend and Sunday School associate into the Council of the Twelve Apostles. Speaking to the general board a few weeks later, Elder McKay said of Elder Richards' appointment to the Twelve, "On that occasion, every mind assented and every heart testified that the Lord had spoken, and that he had indeed called into the service of the apostleship a 'chosen vessel.' "

At that same time, paying tribute to his associate, President McKay continued:

His sincere interest in the great Sunday School cause has been an inspiration to his fellow-workers. His clear judgment and sound reasoning have commanded the respect particularly of the general board, with whom he is closely associated. His loyalty to them and to the cause has won their loyalty to him; his gentlemanly and courteous consideration of their thoughts and feelings, his unselfish devotion to the truth, and his invincible determination to choose the right have merited their abiding confidence and high esteem.

President Richards' health was not the best for many years while he was serving as a member of the Twelve. He suffered greatly at times because of a heart ailment, and we feared at times that his end was near. But following his appointment to the First Presidency he worked harder than ever before, although he occasionally found it necessary in the interest of his health to go away for a brief rest and relaxation. He had the ability to know how to relax when the need seemed the greatest.

This man gave to President McKay and to his position as a counselor in the First Presidency his every ounce of energy, even frequently when he was not well. He was completely devoted to his old friend and to the Church. President McKay relied wholeheartedly on his judgment, particularly in financial and missionary matters, and he leaned heavily upon him.

One of President Richards' favorite themes was the home and family, and he left to posterity and the Church some truly classical discourses on that subject, full of wise counsel and inspiration. He contended that the strength of the community and of the Church depended upon safeguarding the family and the home.

It could be said of President Richards that he literally gave his life in the service of the Church. For many days he had been regularly at the office, when all his friends and the Church were shocked and saddened by his sudden passing from a heart attack on May 19, 1959.

The great respect and love President McKay had for his long-time counselor and confidant was evidenced when he, with much emotion, took final leave of

President Richards in these few brief heartfelt words:
"Goodbye for the present, Stephen L, my beloved
friend and associate. We shall miss you—Oh! how
we shall miss you!—but we shall continue to carry on
until we meet again."

These words found echo in the hearts of all of us
who heard this loving farewell.

PRESIDENT HENRY D. MOYLE

When President David O. McKay moved to fill the
vacancy in the First Presidency occasioned by the death
of Stephen L Richards, he chose Henry D. Moyle,
one of the dynamic and forceful members of the
Council of the Twelve, who had proven abilities of
leadership, loyalty, dedication, and faithfulness.

President Moyle's call to the First Presidency on
June 13, 1959, was as second counselor. President J.
Reuben Clark, Jr., who had faithfully served President
McKay as second counselor for more than eight years,
once more became first counselor in the First Presidency.
Thus President McKay again had two strong, wise
counselors at his right and left hands.

It is interesting to note that President McKay,
himself a noted educator and teacher, had called to
his side as his first three counselors men who, in
addition to their long and faithful Church service, were
trained in and had reached notable heights in the legal
profession. Even his next choice as a counselor in the
First Presidency followed the same pattern when another
noted attorney and churchman, Hugh B. Brown, was
called as a counselor at the time of the death of President Clark.

The appointment of President Moyle to the First
Presidency was a climax to a noteworthy life's career
as student, missionary, lawyer, professor of law, army
officer, eminently successful business executive, national

executive in the petroleum industry, stake president, general chairman of the Church Welfare Committee, and member of the Council of the Twelve.

President Moyle was a man of dynamic personality as well as unwavering faith. His remarkable background, training, and experience as well as his faith in, devotion to, and understanding of the gospel and Church procedures qualified him for the mission he performed as a counselor in the First Presidency. He was an able and influential speaker, and his persuasiveness and example went far in making a success of most every assignment and responsibility given him or in which he took the initiative.

This man brought a welcome vigor and vitality into his new position, permitting him to give valuable assistance and counsel to his associates. His organizational abilities, coming from his legal training and wide business experience, helped him to succeed especially in three areas of responsibility that were, among others, given him by President McKay.

One of these was the missionary program. This had been an area of responsibility very dear to President McKay, who had held it himself for nearly a score of years and in which President Richards had followed through so devotedly. President Moyle had been an energetic and successful missionary in Germany in his younger years. After his missionary service he had remained on for a year to pursue his education at the at the time of the early depression years. At the same this year his missionary work did not cease, and he frequently joined the missionaries in their activities. He was in Germany from 1909 to 1912, years before World War I, and he and his companions often faced persecution and threats of imprisonment.

Now, as a counselor in the First Presidency responsible for missionary work of the Church throughout the world, President Moyle entered into this

assignment with the same zeal and dynamism he gave
to every phase of his life. When he took the direction
of the missionary program, the Church had about
5,000 missionaries in the field. Four years later the
number had increased to 12,000. He had the personality
and capacity to enthuse and inspire mission leaders
and through them imbue the missionaries with confidence and a positive attitude that brought outstanding
results. Convert baptisms began to reach impressive,
almost unheard-of totals. He frequently visited with
mission presidents and missionaries in seminars in
Great Britain, on the European continent, and throughout the United States. His personal influence and
testimony were contagious. He made the missionaries
feel that whatever they set their minds to do, they could
accomplish if they had the Lord on their side.

Second, President Moyle brought into the First
Presidency a firsthand knowledge of the welfare program and all its ramifications. For 20 years he had been
the general chairman of the program. His first identi-
fication with Church welfare was when it had its
small beginning in several stakes of the Salt Lake
Valley. He was presiding over the Cottonwood Stake
at the time of the early depression years. At the same
time President Harold B. Lee was presiding over
Pioneer Stake, and some of the first bishop's storehouse activities were set up by them in their respective
stakes on a pioneering basis.

President Moyle remained as stake president for
ten years beginning in 1927 and was released when he
was appointed by the First Presidency to serve as the
welfare program's second general chairman. In this
office he succeeded Elder Melvin J. Ballard of the
Council of the Twelve, who had passed away after
serving the first year. This new appointment brought
President Moyle into close association with President
Lee, who the year before had been named the program's

first managing director. Four years later, a third prominent Salt Lake churchman was to join with them in giving wise, persistent, and energetic leadership to Church welfare. This third man was Elder Marion G. Romney, who today is a counselor in the First Presidency. President Romney was named one of the first Assistants to the Twelve in April 1941 and almost immediately became the assistant managing director of Church welfare. History has shown that beginning at that time, and for the next score of years, these three were the guiding forces of an inspired program of taking care of the needy and developing initiative and independence among the Church membership. President J. Reuben Clark, Jr., was also closely allied with these three apostles in laying the groundwork and charting the course of the great welfare program.

I am sure the loss of President Moyle's dynamic and confident spirit and dedication to this program was felt keenly by his associates when his early passing came in 1963.

In yet a third area President Moyle's influence and life's training were to be a powerful asset to President McKay. A man of considerable business acumen and experience through association with large industrial and financial concerns, he was entrusted by President McKay with much of the Church's business and financial affairs. These he assumed with his usual dependability, forthrightness, and energy.

One example of his thinking and farsightedness is the Church's large ranch and cattle holdings in Florida. The Deseret Farms of Florida began under his personal direction and supervision, wherein hundreds of thousands of acres of swamp lands and unproductive areas were drained and reclaimed and became one of the great undertakings and assets of the Church.

In everything, President Moyle thought big and had the energy, vision, and determination to follow through. It was during the period of his service in the First Presidency that plans were developed and carried forward initially for the present, newly completed and occupied 28-story high-rise General Church Office Building on the block east of Temple Square in Salt Lake City. It will long remain as a memorial to the enterprising dynamism that characterized this prominent Churchman.

President Moyle was a successful, affluent business executive and lawyer, with influence reaching throughout the Intermountain West, when he was called into the Council of the Twelve in 1947 by President George Albert Smith. From that time on, his entire attention and dedication was to the Church. He traveled widely and was a familiar and well-loved figure throughout the stakes and missions. He was a forceful and interesting speaker, radiating an air of confidence and optimism combined with deep spirituality, humility, and faith that deeply influenced the lives of all who heard him. He was a man most highly respected by all who knew him in the varied circles in which he moved.

His financial wealth was not inherited. He had the ability to fully capitalize on his high educational attainments, for he had on the wall of his office degrees obtained from several noted institutions of higher education, beginning with the University of Utah, from which he was graduated in 1909 with a degree in mining engineering. As previously stated, he studied geology for a year at the University of Freiberg, following his mission. He returned home to reenter the University of Utah, where he received a degree in science and studied law. In 1915 he was awarded a law degree from the University of Chicago. Later he studied for a year at Harvard. For 25 years he was on the law faculty of the University of Utah.

Naming just a few of his industrial achievements will help to portray the great capacity and varied interests of President Moyle—the same abilities to succeed that he brought with him into the First Presidency, making him an able, experienced, and energetic counselor. At one time he was president of the Inland Empire Oil Refinery and the Troy Mining Company and vice-president of the Wasatch Oil Refinery and the Idaho Oil Refinery. He was also president of the Deseret Livestock Co. and a consultant to Phillips Petroleum. He was a member of the board of trustees of the Consolidated Freightways, Inc., and a founder of the Utah Truck Owners' Association, for which he served many years as general counsel. He earned the reputation of being one of the best authorities in the field of transportation in the Mountain West, and during World War II he served his country as one of the government directors of the oil industry. He later became a director of the Petroleum Industry Council and chairman of refining for District Four—the Mountain West states. Following this war-time emergency organization, his abilities were recognized further with his appointment as a director of the more permanent National Petroleum Council

Such were the high temporal achievements of this man who filled such an important place in the presiding councils of the Church. But great as were his business and financial successes, they did not, nor would he ever let them, supercede in interest and devotion his ecclesiastical responsibilities. He used his wealth wisely in service to his fellowmen. The extent of his contributions to worthy causes and to aid his closest friends will never be known, for always he had so stipulated.

To me, perhaps, as I sat so often in the council meetings, the outstanding characteristics of President Moyle were his faith in God, his unquestioned testimony of the latter-day work in which he was engaged, and his unwavering, unquestionable loyalty to Presi-

dent McKay. Of his prophet-leader he often testified
that he was indeed inspired of God.

I have been impressed with the manner in which
President Moyle passed from this life. It was indeed a
peaceful ending, befitting a man who literally wore
himself out in the service of the Master. Though
afflicted with a heart ailment for several years, this
dynamic leader did not spare himself in spending his
energy to the very last for the building up of God's
kingdom on earth.

But even more impressively, his peaceful end came
in his sleep during the night while in a home and place
dear to his heart, the church-owned farm-ranch home
at Deer Park, Florida. This project was largely of his
vision and planning, and he visited it often in the
course of his official duties. He had died as he would
have wished, in the harness and heavily involved in the
greatest of causes, serving the people he loved.

Two nights before his quiet passing he had addressed
a meeting in the nearby Ellsworth Ward chapel. Those
of the official party who accompanied him said he
spoke feelingly of his love of the Church and gave
once again, for the last time, his powerful personal
testimony of the "divine calling of President McKay as
a prophet of God."

So this man of achievement died, as he had lived,
full of faith, love of the gospel and his fellowmen, loyal
to his leaders and associates. He had an undoubting
faith and knowledge that this is the work of the Lord
and that the Master opens the way and guides his
chosen servants in the accomplishment of his purposes,
if they do their part, seeking the inspiration and
guidance of the Holy Spirit.

I have been humbly grateful that the life of such a
fearless and untiring worker has touched my life so
closely. I felt of him that he was such as would give
his all, even his very life, for the advancement of the

cause he so dearly loved. This he did as few men are privileged to do.

PRESIDENT HUGH B. BROWN

As the reader is by now aware, I have seen many men come into high Church service as counselors in the First Presidency. However much I have learned to love and appreciate these men for themselves and for the contributions they have made to the Church, I can say that none came into such position for whom I had a greater personal affection and friendship when his appointment came than President Hugh B. Brown.

I had known him for many years and admired his spiritual fervor and ability to inspire others with his special gift of oratory. But, more than that, he had been, and still is, my very dear friend. My acquaintance with President Brown began many years before he became a General Authority of the Church.

This association and friendship was intensified during 1937 when he was called to preside over the British Mission and in that year President Heber J. Grant went to Europe and I had the pleasure of accompanying him. As we traveled about Europe, President Brown and I became close companions, and since that time my feelings for him have been of love and appreciation. My admiration for him still continues. He is a man the people love and one who loves the people of the Church.

President McKay had had a long acquaintance with Hugh B. Brown during the latter's long and prominent service to the Church as missionary, president of two stakes, twice president of the British Mission, youth leader and Church Servicemen's Coordinator. It was President McKay who called his trusted friend and associate into the ranks of the General Authorities to be an Assistant to the Council of the Twelve in 1953.

He was then advanced to be a member of the Council of the Twelve in 1958 at the age of 74 years. It was also in June of that year that President Brown and his sweetheart, Zina Card Brown, a granddaughter of Brigham Young, celebrated their golden wedding anniversary.

During the presidency of President McKay, at a time when President Clark was advancing in years and the demands upon the First Presidency were growing heavier and heavier as they have over the years, Hugh B. Brown was called from the Council of the Twelve to serve as an additional counselor in the First Presidency. This was in June 1961, and a few months later, in October, when President Clark passed away just after his ninetieth birthday, President Brown became second counselor in the Presidency. President Moyle was advanced to first counselor to succeed President Clark.

All who know President Brown know of his humble faith and the strength of his testimony. Among my acquaintances in the General Authorities during the past 50 years, President Brown has been outstanding in his ability to preach the gospel and influence his listeners. His is a special gift of oratory, and he has always been a mighty preacher of the gospel, as he seeks to share his knowledge and testimony through sermons given throughout the world and through the messages that have come from his gifted pen.

Of course, the power of his exemplary life and his example of Christian virtues have added to the persuasive force of his spoken messages. He has been an outstanding friend-maker for the Church, and these friends include people of nobility and in high places as well as those in lowly walks of life, both members and nonmembers. His great love and devotion for those with whom he has associated cannot be measured, nor can his faith in and appreciation of his fellowmen generally.

As I have been fortunately permitted to do, many people in the Church today have come under the refreshing spell of his delightful personality. His warmth and friendship, his keen sense of humor, his progressive nature and awareness of that which is going on about him make it ever more exciting to listen to him or just to be in his presence.

Typical of his alertness to a changing world about him was his comment when asked by a newsman what his reactions were to being called as a counselor in the First Presidency. He said, "It is quite a shock to be so launched as a missile and thrown into dizzy orbit." Another experience which showed that this man, then at the age of 77 years, was keeping apace of the jet-age world about him was a speech he made about the same time to students of Brigham Young University, which he entitled "Eternal Flight." He said:

You are astronauts . . . launched from another sphere and temporarily on this little space island preparing to continue an endless flight. . . .

You have been provided with a very miraculous space suit or capsule. Each of you has been given a divine spark, which will continue to ignite that super-fuel which we call truth and knowledge —and of this there is an inexhaustible supply. A constant refueling will enable you to continue this second stage of your journey. Then you will launch an indestructible missile, yourself, and propel it into outer space. The amount of the fuel—knowledge—which you acquire and utilize will determine and in a sense delimit your flight.

The advice President Brown gave the students on that occasion was but a page from the formula of his own life. He continues to keep abreast of the world about him by continuing a program of constant reading of the great books of the world. His published sermons and writings of well over a half century of Church service attest to his firm belief in a balanced mental diet. They display a vast knowledge of life and a realistic approach to the gospel that has constantly appealed to young and old alike.

One of his former colleagues, the late Elder Richard

L. Evans, in writing a foreword to one of President
Brown's several books of sermons and writings, gave a
word picture of the author, which reveals the real Hugh
B. Brown as I have known and admired him. Said
Elder Evans:

> His power to touch intimately and forgettably the hearts and
> lives of young people includes encouragement to question freely
> and sincerely—but with faith and with respect for facts, and for
> authority, and for eternal truths.
>
> He is an uncommon man—approachable, lovable, human,
> courageous, forthright, dedicated to lifting lives with a warmth
> that comforts, that encourages, that gives real and solid hope to
> the repentant, the wayward, the wandering; to those who have
> made mistakes, and to those who are sincerely searching and
> seeking.

Truly the eloquence of his sermons and the power
of his testimony have been a strong influence in my
life as well as in the lives of all who have heard him,
whether from the pulpit, in the classroom, or in the
intimate councils of the brethren. He will always be
remembered by me as one of God's noblemen. His
has been a noble service over a period of many years,
beginning as a missionary to Great Britain in his early
youth. This began a tie between Hugh B. Brown and
the British people that was to endure for many years.

Though born in Salt Lake City, he moved early with
his family to Alberta, Canada, where he spent his earlier
years working on farms, ranches, canals, and railroads.
Always giving faithful service to the Church, he was
named in 1921 as president of the Lethbridge Stake,
this appointment coming after service in the bishopric
and on the Alberta Stake high council. He moved to Salt
Lake City with his family in 1927 to take up the
practice of law, for which he had completed legal training
at the University of Alberta. The services of this experienced leader were soon to be required by his
Church, when the next year he became president of the
Granite Stake in Salt Lake City.

It was in 1937 that he left to preside over the British Mission, remaining there until 1940, when he aided in the evacuation of missionaries from Europe at the start of World War II.

Because of his experiences and capacity to reach young people, President Brown was named Church servicemen's coordinator during the war years, directing their spiritual training and counseling hundreds of men and women in uniform. He continued this activity until 1944, when he was again called to preside over the British Mission in the immediate post-war-years.

Returning home to Salt Lake City in 1946, he joined the faculty of Brigham Young University, where he became one of the most popular teachers of religion and also continued to coordinate servicemen's activities.

He had returned to Canada to resume his law practice and was just beginning a successful business career when the long arm of inspired Church authority, as it so often does, reached out to again call him into service. He was summoned by President McKay in 1953 to be an Assistant to the Council of the Twelve, and in 1958 was advanced to be a member of the Council of the Twelve.

He served President McKay loyally and devotedly with wise counsel born of a life rich in experience, devotion, righteousness, and faith. When President McKay passed away in January 1970, President Brown graciously resumed his former place of seniority in the Council of the Twelve, where he continues to enjoy the love and appreciation of his associates, though ill health and advancing years do not permit him to be as active as his faithful spirit would dictate.

It should be said of President Brown that he has taken an extremely active part, under President McKay's leadership, in moving forward the construction of the Washington, D.C., temple. He dedicated the temple site in 1969, breaking ground at the same time, and worked closely with the Church leaders in the nation's capital to begin the fund drives and construction work of the temple. At this writing it is one of his fondest hopes that he will be able to attend the temple's dedication scheduled for sometime in the summer of 1974. This, he feels, would be a fitting climax to his life of service in the work of the Master.

As I think of the influence on my life of President Brown and of the many, many lives he has touched in his long, rewarding service to his fellowmen, especially the youth, I think of words penned by him in 1948 and appearing as a preface to his book *Continuing the Quest.* Entitled "Raw Materials," this message reveals the heart and soul of a devoted servant:

As the violinist tunes each string until it responds with an individual tone, capable of harmonious response to a master's hand;

As Handel and Mendelssohn placed symbols on paper which, when combined with poetic images, became oratorios:

As Cicero and Demosthenes used words with such discriminating skill as to make each one do its best and express an exact meaning and then wove them into great orations;

As Milton and Shakespeare arranged incidents into immortal dramas and poetry;

As Lincoln and Churchill held aloft ideals and inspired their countrymen to save their nations;

So let us try to touch the lives of young men and women; to inspire each to do and be his best, to know that he is unique in God's handiwork and that his contribution is required in the immortal symphony—thus may we help create from life's raw materials something beautiful and everlasting and do it with the throbbing, pulsating, malleable souls of God's children and help him to achieve his avowed purpose—immortality and eternal life for all.

—H.B.B., Provo, 1948.

PRESIDENT NATHAN ELDON TANNER

I count myself very fortunate indeed to have had President Nathan Eldon Tanner come into my life as he did 13 years ago. I knew of him and the successful leadership he was giving to the Calgary Stake in Canada, but I had no personal acquaintance with him until he was named an Assistant to the Council of the Twelve in October 1960 and moved to Salt Lake City.

His appointment as a General Authority and subsequent remarkable contribution of inspired leadership in the presiding councils of the Church is but further evidence to me that the Lord has in constant preparation men to call into these high positions at the right time. As I have become personally well acquainted with President Tanner and know of his background and life's experiences, I am well aware of how thorough was that preparation. From very humble beginnings he molded a career in Canada that brought remarkable achievements in varied fields, including public service, industry, finance, education, and business. These heights he achieved without sacrifice of his spiritual ideals and standards or his dedicated, devoted service to the Church.

I have become even better acquainted with President Tanner since his call into the First Presidency ten years ago. In these few years he has wielded a wonderful influence upon my life. He is a man of great faith and testimony, of dedication to the highest principles of integrity and honesty, a man of practical and inspired vision, blessed abundantly with common sense and the courage of his convictions.

President Tanner's advancement within the presiding councils of the Church has been rapid indeed. He served but two years as an Assistant to the Twelve, and much of that time as president of the newly created West European Mission with headquarters in London. This mission comprised all the areas of England, Scotland, Wales, and Ireland, two missions in France, and the Netherlands. His call to this assignment came only four days after he had traveled to England in company with

President McKay and President Brown for the purpose
of dedicating the Hyde Park Chapel in London and
organizing the London Stake.

In 1962 he was named to the Council of the
Twelve, and a year later President McKay selected him
as second counselor in the First Presidency. His public
response on being sustained to this position was typical
of the humble dedication of his life. He said, "I humbly
thank you all for your confidence and sustaining vote,
and pledge to you and to God himself everything with
which the Lord has blessed me for the building up of
the kingdom of God."

In the First Presidency, President Tanner succeeded
to the vacancy occasioned by the death of President
Moyle.

For the next seven years Hugh B. Brown and N.
Eldon Tanner served as first and second counselors to
President McKay. During that time, and many times
since, both of these great, sincere men have extended
to me their confidence and love in a remarkable manner.
Had I been an associate counselor with them, they
could not have treated me with more kindness and
deference. I have been with President Tanner on many
occasions when he has demonstrated his sincere love of
the gospel and his love for and devotion to the president
of the Church. Both President Brown and President
Tanner have indicated to me on various occasions, and
I know they have been sincere, that they would gladly
have given their lives, if necessary, for President McKay.

Knowing President Tanner as I do, I am aware that
he manifested the same love and loyal devotion to President Joseph Fielding Smith, whom he continued to
serve as second counselor, and today he is a tower of
strength with the same loyalty, devotion, and dedication
as first counselor to our beloved leader, President
Harold B. Lee.

President Tanner is one of only four men in the

history of the Church who have served as a counselor to three or more presidents of the Church. To each of these presidents he has been and is extremely loyal. Possessed of unusual abilities and qualifications for his high position, he has been and is today a trusted, devoted, and wise counselor.

I shall always hold President Tanner in the highest esteem because of his steadiness in service, his humble faith in the Lord, and his oft-expressed sincere, yet simple, testimony of the gospel. I have great respect for his strength of character. My experiences with him have revealed him to be a man of honor and integrity, trustworthy in every aspect of his life. He is kind, considerate, and approachable, with a love for his fellowmen regardless of their position in life. He has a forthright, fearless, practical approach to the problems of life and to the responsibilities of his high office. He possesses a keen sense of humor and an innate friendliness that draw people to him.

He has a deep interest in and love for the youth of the Church. Having associated much of his life with young people as a schoolteacher, as a Boy Scout leader, and for many years as a branch president and bishop, he understands them and their problems. They find him easy to approach and willing to listen and to help solve their problems. Typical of his effectiveness with youth is an incident related about him in a recent issue of the *Ensign*, written by his associate and revered uncle, President Brown. After telling of Eldon Tanner's first experiences as a schoolteacher in a three-room school in Hill Spring, Canada, President Brown wrote:

President Tanner next took a position as high school teacher in Cardston and moved his family there. During his eight years in Cardston he was on the town council, principal of an elementary school, scoutmaster, bishop's counselor and later bishop of the Cardston First Ward.

His humility and leadership ability were shown by his actions while serving as a counselor in the bishopric and adviser to the deacons quorum. Some of the boys were not attending their meetings. He soon discovered the reason as he visited them in their homes. They had no Sunday clothes and were embarrassed to wear their overalls. The following Sunday, according to agreement with the boys, he met with them at priesthood meeting in overalls. Needless to say he won the love of those young boys and they were soon 100 percent active.

He still maintains a similar rapport with the young people as he speaks to them and as they visit him frequently in his office.

Dependability is another of the outstanding characteristics of President Tanner. From his early youth, being the oldest child in the family, he learned to accept responsibility. As a young boy he drove a four-horse team hauling grain. He learned to work hard and grew to manhood with the strength of character and independence so often resulting from a close relationship with nature and the out-of-doors and the constant struggle to win a livelihood from the soil.

He had a great love and respect for his pioneering parents, Nathan William and Edna Brown Tanner, who homesteaded in the area of Aetna, Canada, having gone there from Salt Lake City by covered wagon. His mother returned to Salt Lake City to give birth to her first child and then took him back to Canada when he was about six weeks old, where his first home was a dugout, a one-room home cut out of a hillside on the family's homestead.

In addition to being taught the value of work and the lessons of dependability and honesty, President Tanner recalls often the lessons of spirituality, love of the gospel, and appreciation for the powers of the holy priesthood that were learned well from these hard-working, deeply religious parents. He was permitted to participate in religious experiences in his home and witnessed the miraculous healing of the sick in answer to his youthful sincere and humble prayers.

On the foundation of these early teachings and experiences, he built a life of successful achievement. He rose to unusual heights of leadership and influence in the Province of Alberta. From the humble position of the town council in Cardston he rose politically to become speaker of the Alberta legislature during his first term, and to appointment of cabinet position as Minister of Lands and Mines for the province, which was later expanded to include the portfolios of Minerals and Forests.

He met the many challenges of conservation and legislation resulting from this high government responsibility, and then several years later he resigned his government position to become president of Merrill Petroleum, Ltd., moving his family to Calgary. Two years later he was induced to become head of the Trans-Canada Pipelines, Ltd., which was in the process of building a 2,200-mile-long pipeline across Canada from Alberta to Montreal. One of the considerations of his acceptance of this responsibility was that he remain in Calgary to establish his headquarters instead of going to Toronto as was intended. The reason was his recent appointment as president of the new Calgary Stake. Since the Church was always first in his life, he was not willing to leave his new assignment of spiritual responsibility. No matter where his frequent travels took him, he always returned to his stake responsibilities on weekends.

After the successful completion of the huge pipeline project, he resigned as the chairman of the company's board in 1958, and for the next two years he served as president of the Canadian Gas Association. He was holding these two important positions—president of the Calgary Stake and of the gas association, when called by President McKay to be a General Authority in 1960.

I have purposely not listed all of President Tanner's

business, educational, and industrial achievements, because this is not intended to be a biography. I have included only enough to show the extent of his achievements in community, religious, financial, and industrial affairs to emphasize his qualifications for his present position in the First Presidency and the special leadership he is now giving under assignment of President Lee to the financial and business affairs of the Church.

I have always enjoyed being in the presence of President Tanner. He is unassuming, friendly, frank, and open and draws from a vast well of practical experience and down-to-earth wisdom and understanding. There has passed through my hands a little booklet entitled *Tannerisms*. It is a compilation of sayings of President Tanner that was compiled by his missionaries in England to remind them of the practical wisdom of their inspired leader. A few of these taken at random reveal the secret of success of President Tanner, for as he taught, so he has lived:

"Rivet your mind to the task at hand."

"If you want your dreams to come true—wake up."

"Discipline—To progress, to become what you want to be and to serve the Lord the way you should, requires that you discipline yourself constantly. Discipline yourself while in your youth so that it will become a habit that will sustain you in later years."

"Every problem is another step upwards. It is a privilege and opportunity to overcome these problems and move upward."

"If you want to be happy, do what the Lord asks you to do."

"The people who object to rules are people who don't obey them."

"Thinking big is thinking that which is important."

"You should take home the very best person your suit will hold."

"Don't depreciate yourself—the Lord will make you equal to your calling no matter who you are if you will put yourself in his hands."

"We have the spark of divinity that enables us to reach unlimited heights."

"The greatest thing that stops the Lord's work is our fear of what other people think."

"When we are in tune with the Lord we have great spiritual experiences."

"The world is divided into two groups—you and the rest of the world; and of the two you are the most important because it is you that works out your salvation, your exaltation, and your eternal life."

"If you follow the authorities' advice in the Church, you will never go wrong."

"Overcome fear by doing what you are afraid to do."

"Learn how to give up as much as you take."

"Have you ever seen a tomorrow? Today is the only day you have to work with."

"Be unselfish. Do not work for credit."

There are many more such statements of wisdom born of experience and understanding, but these are sufficient to reveal the humanness and sound practical approach to life of a great leader. I shall always be humbly grateful for the inspiration that directed President McKay to reach out into southern Alberta and bring into my life and into the important affairs of God's kingdom a man such as President Tanner. He is making and will continue to make, in his position next to President Lee, an outstanding contribution to the fast-growing kingdom of God. May the Lord continue to bless and inspire him for many years yet to come.

SECTION FOUR

Leadership of President Joseph Fielding Smith

7

President Smith, A Man Of Powerful Testimony

No one I ever knew among the General Authorities of the Church in the past 50 years bore a more impressive and certain testimony of the gospel of Jesus Christ than did President Joseph Fielding Smith, tenth president of the Church. It was a testimony always borne in simplicity and conviction. Its simplicity matched his life, as also did its humbleness of expression. It was a testimony rich in a heritage of priceless family tradition.

Of a surety it was his own testimony. The conviction that God lives and that he was engaged in the true and everlasting gospel of Jesus Christ as restored in the earth in our day was in his own heart. This knowledge influenced his whole life and manner of living. He lived the principles of the gospel in his life because he truly believed them to be the true pathway to exaltation. He fearlessly proclaimed them from the pulpit, far and wide, because of the divine admonition so to do as a "special witness of Jesus Christ to all the world."

President Smith was one of those noble men of God who were numbered among the Twelve Apostles when I began my work for the president and the

First Presidency in 1922. He had already served one-fifth of the time he was to be a member of the Council of the Twelve—a total of 60 years.

That his call to the apostleship and eventually to the position of president of the Church was a

President Joseph Fielding Smith called as his counselors in the First Presidency in 1970 President Harold B. Lee, right, and President N. Eldon Tanner, left.

part of the Lord's plan for his earthly sojourn before he was born is amply evident. When he was 19 years of age, his uncle, John Smith, gave him a blessing in which he said, among other things:

It shall be thy duty to sit in counsel with thy brethren, and to preside among the people. It shall be thy duty also to travel much at home and abroad, by land and water, laboring in the ministry . . . and the blessings of the Lord shall rest upon thee. His spirit shall direct thy mind and give thee word and sentiment, that thou shalt confound the wisdom of the wicked and set at naught the counsels of the unjust.

As I think back, I recall that many years ago Sister Noah S. Pond, who was a relative of Joseph Fielding Smith, told me that on one occasion when she was a young girl and was at a party where Brother Smith was also present, a voice very distinctly told her that someday that young man would be the president of the Church. I recall that when she related this to me, I also had the burning assurance in my own soul that this would be the case. As I associated over the years with President Smith, learned to know the purity of his heart, heard his burning testimony, and felt the majesty of his soul, this assurance not only remained but grew stronger and stronger. I was certain that he was destined to become our prophet and president. I must confess, however, that when he became 92 years of age and then 93, I wondered if I was mistaken.

I rejoiced with the rest of those who knew and loved this humble, worthy leader when the call came in the first month of 1970, in the same year when, on July 19, he would observe his ninety-fourth birthday. Though he presided over the Church for only two and one-half years, they were eventful years; many great things were accomplished under his presidency as the horizons of the Church's influence

and responsibility were pushed farther and farther
on the earth, and important and far-reaching
changes were wrought.

President Heber J. Grant told me of the conditions
surrounding the selection and appointment of Joseph
Fielding Smith to become a member of the Council
of the Twelve in April 1910.

He said Joseph Fielding Smith, son of President
Joseph F. Smith, who had nominated him for the
position, was unanimously approved by the Council
of the Twelve without reservation. Inasmuch as one
of President Smith's sons, Hyrum M. Smith, was
already a member of the Twelve at the time, and
another son, David A. Smith, was a member of
the Presiding Bishopric, there was considerable
discussion among the people about this matter.
Some claimed that Joseph was called by relationship
rather than by revelation, but his life and his work
verified that he was most certainly called of God to
this high position.

President Smith was a vigorous and courageous
defender of the truths of the gospel. His forthrightness in speaking and teaching and fearless denun-
ciation of false doctrines expounded by men stemmed
from his unexcelled knowledge of the word of
the Lord in the holy scriptures. One visiting his
office over the many years would invariably find
him reading the scriptures or discussing the gospel
with a visitor sitting across the desk from him,
or he would be seated at his own typewriter com-
posing answers to the many questions on doctrine
and Church history received by him.

He said at a general conference soon after being
named as president of the Church:

All my life I have studied the scriptures, and have sought
the guidance of the Spirit of the Lord in coming to an understanding
of their true meaning. The Lord has been good to me and I rejoice

in the knowledge he has given me and in the privilege that has been and is mine to teach his saving truths. . . . What I have taught and written in the past I would teach and write again under the same circumstances.

He was perhaps the most prolific writer on Church doctrine, history, and policy that we have had. He was a great scripturalist and an able and qualified preacher of the gospel. He spoke at all times as one having authority and complete understanding. His writings and sermons stressed the basics of the gospel. His was most frequently a call to repentance. He did this with a seriousness and intensity that often brought criticism that he was brusque, severe, and abrupt in manner. It was always evident to him that preaching the gospel was a serious matter. But this apparent brusqueness covered up a very natural shyness, warmth, understanding, and sympathetic nature, always evident to those who knew him well.

I knew President Smith when he was a rather young man, and I listened to him almost with awe at various times in the council meetings discussing with others of the Council of the Twelve matters of doctrine about which there was a difference of opinion. His statements carried with them at all times the ring of authority and of truth. He was, in very deed, a tireless worker and a devout and thorough student and defender of the truth.

To me, President Smith was a man without guile. In his entire life he surely avoided the very appearance of evil. He hated evil, but he was truly and remarkably considerate of the sinner if he showed any signs of repentance. I have heard people who knew him well say that if they were to be judged for any transgression or error by any of the General Authorities here or in the hereafter and could have their choice, Joseph Fielding Smith would be the man they would choose. He was always fair and honest, above reproach in his own life, kindly, sympathetic, and loving. He was untiring in urging people to repent and live righteous lives.

His sense of humor was contagious and spontaneous, but his laughter was never boisterous. He felt that the gospel was a source of real happiness and joy to mankind, but he had some fundamental views on amusements, expressed once in his writings as follows:

> I believe it is necessary for the Saints to have amusements, but of the proper kind. I do not believe the Lord intends and desires that we should pull a long face and look sanctimonious and hypocritical.
>
> I think he expects us to be happy and of cheerful countenance, but he does not expect of us the indulgence in boisterous and unseemly conduct and the seeking after vain and foolish things which amuse and entertain the world. He has commanded us to the contrary for our own good and eternal welfare. We should not get the idea from scripture that the Lord is displeased with us when we laugh, when we have merriment, if it is on the right occasion.

President Smith possessed a modern, questing spirit and had a love of life right up to the end of his mortal existence. One writer said, "President Smith's life began in the 19th century and ended in the 20th century, and his outlook and insights grew with the times to span nearly 100 years of progress."

It was well known that President Smith was adopted by the Utah National Guard, becoming an "honorary brigadier general," and that in his adventurous spirit he delighted to fly as a passenger in a jet fighter plane. It is told of him that on one occasion when other appointments made it seem likely that he would miss a conference assignment on Sunday in the San Francisco area, a young jet pilot friend in the National Guard learned of this

The author, right, pictured with President Joseph Fielding Smith of the Council of the Twelve, at laying of cornerstone of Oakland Temple. Elder O. Leslie Stone, chairman of the temple district, and later an Assistant to the Twelve, is at the left.

and told President Smith that his plane crew was lacking some air time for the month and that the trip to the Bay Area and back was about the distance they needed. President Smith accepted the invitation without hesitation, and the appointment was kept. President Smith even rounded up most of the plane's crew and took them with him to Sunday conference in San Francisco.

While he enjoyed relaxation and recreation, sports in particular, both as a fan and participant, his devotion to the basic principles that governed his life kept him from countenancing recreation on Sunday. He said as Church president, "The modern problem of our day that stands out in my mind is keeping the Sabbath day. When we fail to keep the Sabbath, we tend to neglect other principles and practices of the gospel."

I have always been keenly aware of President Smith's love of life. He had a zest for living and appreciation of the world about him. Perhaps one of the best expressions of his love of life was written by the late Elder Richard L. Evans, one of his colleagues among the General Authorities. He wrote:

We see Brother Smith as the father and grandfather and husband of many talents and of much devotion—as the father who attends the bedside of the sick, who performs early and late, at all hours, many kindly services, who counsels with his own and others on personal problems, school problems, social problems, spiritual problems.

There are also those who know him as a confiding friend and counselor in his office. There are those who know him as a storyteller of impressive sincerity. And there are even some who know him as the 'baby sitter', which he has been for his children and his children's children. There are those who know the quickness of his humor, the tenderness of his heart, the sympathy of his soul.

He loves life, and he has shown by his life that he loves truth, that he loves the Church, and that he loves his Father's children. And he is, in turn, . . . admired and respected . . . for his sterling qualities of character, and for himself.

President Smith assumed the presidency of the Church in January 1970 upon the death of his lifelong friend and associate, President McKay. The first opportunity he had to address the Church was at the April conference of that year. In his opening address he sounded what might well have been considered the platform of his period of leadership. He told the world at this conference:

We believe in the dignity and divine origin of man. Our faith is founded on the fact that God is our Father, and that we are his children, and that all men are brothers and sisters in the same eternal family.

As members of his family, we dwelt with him before the foundations of this earth were laid, and he ordained and established the plan of salvation whereby we gained the privilege of advancing and progressing as we are endeavoring to do.

The God we worship is a glorified Being in whom all power and perfection dwell, and he has created man in his own image and likeness, with those characteristics and attributes which he himself possesses.

And so our belief in the dignity and destiny of man is an essential part both of our theology and of our way of life. It is the very basis of our Lord's teaching that "the first and great commandment" is: "Thou shalt love the Lord thy God with all thy heart, and with all thy soul, and with all thy mind"; and the second great commandment is: "Thou shalt love thy neighbour as thyself." (Matt. 22:37-39)

Because God is our Father, we have a natural desire to love and serve him and to be worthy members of his family. We feel an obligation to do what he would have us do, to keep his commandments and live in harmony with the standards of his gospel—all of which are essential parts of true worship.

And because all men are brothers, we have a desire to love and bless and fellowship them—and this too we accept as an essential part of true worship.

Thus everything we do in the Church centers around the divine law that we are to love and worship God and serve our fellowmen.

In this initial address, President Smith, with quiet dignity and firm fearlessness, spoke out against some of the evils of the day, including social and cultural trends in immorality, and against the spirit of disruption typified in riots and campus upheavals. He expressed great concern for the spiritual and moral welfare of the youth everywhere, saying, "Morality, chastity, virtue, freedom from sin—these are and must be basic to our way of life, if we are to realize its full purpose."

At the time of his appointment, he selected two stalwarts as his counselors, Harold B. Lee as first counselor and Nathan Eldon Tanner as second counselor. At this same conference, which included the solemn assembly in which the First Presidency, Council of the Twelve, and Patriarch to the Church were sustained by special voting procedure, which follows the naming of a new Church president,

President Smith paid special tribute to his counselors, saying:

When my father, President Joseph F. Smith, was called to serve as the sixth president of the Church, he expressed gratitude for his devoted counselors and declared his intention to counsel with them in all matters pertaining to the Church, that there might be a oneness and unity among the brethren and before the Lord.

Now may I say that I have complete confidence in my counselors. They are men of God who are guided by the inspiration of heaven. They enjoy the gift and power of the Holy Ghost and have no desires other than to further the interests of the Church and to bless our Father's children, and perfect the work of the Lord on earth.

President Harold B. Lee is a pillar of truth and righteousness, a true seer who has great spiritual strength and insight and wisdom, and whose knowledge and understanding of the Church and its needs is not surpassed by any man.

President N. Eldon Tanner is a man of like caliber, of perfect integrity, of devotion to truth, who is endowed with that administrative ability and spiritual capacity which enables him to lead and counsel and direct aright.

There are many, many other facets of the life of President Smith that I might continue to describe with profit, such as his great church service in genealogy and temple work, with which he was prominently identified since the beginning of the Genealogical Society, and his great service, since serving as a young returned missionary from Great Britain, to the Historical Department. He was named an assistant Church Historian in 1906 and in 1921 became Church Historian and Recorder, which position he held for half a century. No one has contributed greater service to compiling and writing Church history. His *Essentials in Church History,* published in 26 editions since its first printing in 1922, has become one of the most widely used volumes of Church literature outside the standard works. His 24 published books on Church history, doctrine, and scriptural interpretation established him as one of the most prolific writers of the Church.

I feel it important as I near the close of this chapter to write of the great heritage of this beloved leader. In his veins flowed the blood of martyrs for the kingdom of God. It was his grandfather, Hyrum Smith, and his great-uncle, the Prophet Joseph Smith, who gave their lives to seal their testimonies of the divine restoration of the gospel of Jesus Christ in this dispensation.

When the Lord revealed by revelation the divine call of Hyrum Smith to be a "prophet and a seer, and a revelator unto my Church, as well as my servant Joseph," he said, in section 124, verse 96, of the Doctrine and Covenants, that "my servant Hyrum may bear record of the things which I shall show unto him, that his name may be had in honorable remembrance from generation to generation, forever and ever."

President Smith's father, Joseph F. Smith, was one of the sons of Hyrum Smith, and after surviving the hardships and persecutions of Nauvoo, he came as a boy of nine with his widowed mother across the plains to the Great Salt Lake Valley. This young boy who drove an ox team across the plains became the sixth president of the Church and one of the greatest exponents of the gospel of Jesus Christ in this dispensation.

The son, President Joseph Fielding Smith, who became the tenth president of the Church, had great love for his father. He often said that he learned the principles of the gospel and a great appreciation of the lives of Joseph and Hyrum Smith at the feet of a loving father. He ever remained true to his noble heritage.

During the closing years of his administration, President McKay called Joseph Fielding Smith to serve as one of his counselors, at the same time retaining his office of President of the Council of Twelve. Most of this time as we went to the Hotel Utah apartment of President McKay, it was my pleasure almost always to accompany President Smith from the Church Administration Building to the Hotel Utah. He would call for me or I would call for him.

Personally, I had a sincere love and affection for President Smith. I feel sure he reciprocated that love, for he expressed it to me on various occasions. He was the president of the Church, the mouthpiece of the Lord, when I was chosen in April 1970 to serve as an Assistant to the Council of the Twelve, and I know that he was a man of God who served under the spirit of inspiration and revelation. His life and service have been a constant assurance to me over the years that the Lord knows whom he wants to preside over his Church, and he never makes a mistake.

SECTION FIVE

Leadership of President Harold B. Lee

8

President Harold B. Lee— The Man of the Hour

As this book is published Harold B. Lee, eleventh president of the Church and the fifth Church leader under whom I have served, is completing his first year in this high office. Already the Church feels the impact and force of his dynamic and inspired leadership, of which I have been personally aware for the past 32 years.

President Lee is the first one I was privileged to observe come into the Council of the Twelve and then rise to the position of seniority where he became a year ago the senior apostle of the Church and the successor of Joseph Fielding Smith as "Prophet, Seer and Revelator, and President of the Church."

Privileged as I have been to serve as secretary to the Council of the First Presidency and the Quorum of the Twelve it is but natural to become well acquainted with these brethren, form personal opinions, and make my own judgments on their special abilities, qualifications and attitudes. Almost weekly I heard their reports, listened to their comments and discussions, and marveled at the expressions of their wise viewpoints on the wide variety of subjects that are considered.

On becoming the eleventh Church President in 1972, President Harold B. Lee called as his counselors, President N. Eldon Tanner, left, and President Marion G. Romney, right.

As I have thus listened to and observed President Lee over the years he has impressed me as being a man of great physical and moral courage. He has always had the courage of his convictions and is not fearful of expressing them. He has always demonstrated great faith in the gospel of Jesus Christ and in the leadership of the Church. He has a remarkable memory. His retention of things that have happened in the past, of actions taken, expressions made by the brethren is almost uncanny.

President Lee is a thorough student of the scriptures. He has a great knowledge and understanding of them, and his memory pertaining thereto is unusually remarkable and reliable.

As the title of this chapter expresses, I truly

regard President Lee as the man of the hour where the Church and its present needs are concerned. For the Church it is a day of world growth with all its demanding challenges, and President Lee, with his abundant personal strength, wisdom, experience, and deep spirituality, is one who can meet the leadership requirements of the time.

Perhaps it is not so unusual to have me say this, for I have felt strongly over the past half century that the Lord always has the right man at the right time as the earthly head of his church, one whom he has prepared and proven through years of experience and who has come through trial and tribulation and is tested and not found wanting.

The Lord's preparation of his present-day prophet-leader has been thorough, covering the period of President Lee's lifetime. First he was born of humble circumstances, to parents who exemplified the highest and truest of Christian virtues, who were deeply spiritual and placed before all else the principles of the gospel and the work of the Lord.

President Lee was born in a small Idaho community—Clifton—and grew to manhood on the family farm where he assumed his full share of responsibilities while pursuing his education in the small country schools, one of which he later was to preside over as a young principal-teacher. This worthy son of the soil learned well the lessons of independence, thrift, hard work, fair play, and honesty which seem to go hand-in-hand with the rugged individualism of farm life, strong family ties, and religious upbringing.

Then came the missionary years which were crowned with successful activities and the beginnings of leadership training.

Further years, which included presiding over a stake of Zion, serving as a civic official and as a school principal in Salt Lake City, were to add to that preparation for greater things to come. During these years, President Lee was also developing his leadership qualities and organizational abilities. For the past several years President Lee has also had the rare privilege of close acquaintance and association of some of the nation's foremost industrial, financial, and business leaders. As he served with these men on boards of directors and national committees and, while making his own contributions in these assignments, the Church leader has acquired much from the wisdom, experience, and vision of these men. He has earned their respect for his own wisdom and sound principles, but even of more value he has given these men in high places of business and government a greater respect for our Church and its principles and tenats.

The Church today is reaping the rewards of President Lee's preparation and skills as an organizer. His practical wisdom is being applied in perfecting reorganizations and strengthening processes which make more effective the overall Church leadership in meeting the needs of a fast-growing, greatly expanding world organization. The calling of Regional Representatives of the Twelve and organizing the far-flung reaches of the Church into regions where every member of the Church, whether in wards of stakes or branches of missions, will have available to them the same programs and opportunities for leadership training, are programs which today are monuments to the vision and organizational abilities of President Lee.

I shall always be grateful for the blessed privilege I have had over the many years to associate with President Lee. This association has also often been outside my official capacity and has touched the social and intimate. We and our wives have belonged to a Church social and study club for many years which greatly increased our personal friendship.

In our study hours all of us have always had the highest regard for the opinions, explanations, gospel interpretations, and dissertations of this man of understanding. His answers to questions have always been enlightening, inspiring, and convincing, leaving no room for doubt or disagreement.

President Lee has always manifested a willingness to discuss gospel principles and at the time of this writing he accepts with inspired confidence the challenge of a doctrinal question or the discussion of religious philosophy. These become evident in his responses as he addresses youth groups of the Church or holds press interviews or conferences. He demonstrates his unusually broad understanding of the gospel as he still continues with an almost weekly question and answer session with companies of new missionaries. He meets them on Monday mornings in the Assembly Room of the Salt Lake Temple just minutes after they have completed their first endowment session and have questions concerning the temple ceremonies and other related points of doctrine. I hope the missionaries fully appreciate this sacred privilege of an intimate appearance before them of God's chosen servant and the inspired wisdom of his timely advice and counsel.

At the risk of sounding repetitious I say that President Lee has always manifested the qualities of true leadership. Those privileged to know him as have I, have marveled at his wisdom and at the strength of his testimony of the truth and validity of the work entrusted to the church of Jesus Christ, of which he is now the earthly head. We have been awed by his great courage, his remarkable memory, his unusual abilities, and particularly his deep spirituality and thorough dedication to the work of the Lord and Master.

President Lee not only has a great love for the Church, but manifests an abundance of love for his fellowmen. He has said and indicated in his own life that "the great power that will save us is the power of love." It is his philosophy that "there is always some way to a man's-heart." He is untiring in the service he renders and does not hesitate in helping those in need of his assistance and blessings. Many who have come to him for administration have had occasion to feel of his deep spirituality. He lives close to the Lord and the Master recognizes his ministrations in a remarkable way.

Out of President Lee's love for his fellowmen has developed an unusual spirit of unity and love among the authorities of the Church. All of us sense this as he has assumed leadership responsibilities and all of us have been brought more and more into his confidence. One of his innovations has been a monthly meeting in the Salt Lake Temple of all of the General Authorities of the Church. These meetings become heart-warming, spiritual experiences, and an opportunity for all to be instructed and counseled uniformly in the current programs, goals, and challenges of the Church.

I personally can testify to the great spirit of unity and oneness which exists among the presiding authorities and of their great love for the membership of the Church. No one among them manifests that love for the members everywhere more than does President Lee. He gave particular expression to such feelings in his closing remarks at the October, 1972 general conference, the first conference over which he presided as president of the Church. He said:

And so I come to you in these closing moments; and as one who is as a patriarch to the Church holding this position, I have a right to extend a blessing to you. I am not concerned about how much you remember in words of what has been said here. I am concerned about how it has made you feel. What are you going to take back with you when you go? What are you going to give to your members and to your wards and stakes and missions?

If you can catch the spirit of what has gone on here during this conference and can feel that great unity now, then take to them my love and blessing. Assure them that the presidency of the Church and the General Authorities really love the members of the Church everywhere, the lowly, the mighty, the educated, the uneducated, wherever they are. Will you please assure them of our love and our concern about them and their welfare.

There has come to me in these last few days a deepening and reassuring faith. I can't leave this conference without saying to you that I have a conviction that the Master hasn't been absent from us on these occasions. This is his Church. Where else would he rather be than right here at the headquarters of his Church? He isn't an absentee master; he is concerned about us. He wants us to follow where he leads. I know that he is a living reality, as is our Heavenly Father. I know it. I only hope that I can qualify for the high place to which he has called me and in which you have sustained me.

I know with all my soul that these sayings are true, and as a special witness I want you to know from the bottom of my heart that there is no shadow of doubt as to the genuineness of the work of the Lord in which we are engaged, the only name under heaven by which mankind can be saved.

My love goes out to my own family, to my associates, to all within the sound of my voice, even the sinners; I would wish that we would reach out to them, and those who are inactive, and bring them into the fold before it is too late.

God be with you. I have the same feeling as perhaps the Master had when he bid goodbye to the Nephites. He said he perceived that they were weak, but if they would go to their homes and ponder what he said, he would come again and instruct them on other occasions. So likewise, you cannot absorb all that you have heard and that we have talked about, but go to your homes now and remember what you can, and get the spirit of what has been done and said, and when you come again, or we come to you, we will try to help you further with your problems. *(Ensign,* January 1973, p. 134.)

In his lifetime President Lee has undergone trials that would severely try the faith of men of weaker fiber, but he has always kept close to the Lord, sought his help in prayer, and indicated an assurance on his part that all things work together for the good of him who serves the Lord. These trials have included the loss of loved ones. For their lives he has pleaded long and fervently, but in the end, he has found the courage and faith to accept the divine verdict that has taken them from him.

Attention of the First Presidency and others of the General Authorities was first attracted to the leadership and abilities of this man when he was a young stake president facing some of the greatest trials and problems of his life. At 31 years of age he had become the president of Pioneer Stake in Salt Lake City—the youngest stake president in the Church. This was in 1930, when this nation and the world were experiencing the great depression.

He presided over a stake whose membership consisted primarily of the families of wage earners, men who worked for railroads, smelters, refineries, factories. He found that more than half of his stake families were totally or partially unemployed.

Elder Gordon B. Hinckley of the Council of Twelve caught the full pathos of the young stake president's feelings and experiences in a recent article on President Lee appearing in the *Ensign* of November 1972:

> Here was a challenge, a terrifying challenge for the young stake president. He worried, he wept, he prayed, as he saw men, once proud and prosperous, reduced through unemployment to a point where they could not feed their families. Then came inspiration to establish a storehouse where food and commodities could be gathered and from which they could be dispersed to the needy. Work projects were undertaken, not only to improve the community, but, more importantly, to afford men an opportunity to work for what they received. An old business building was demolished and the materials were used to construct a stake gymnasium to provide social and recreational facilities for the people.

Elder Hinckley went on to explain that other stakes were engaged in similar projects, and in April 1936, under the leadership of President Grant, these were coordinated to form what was first called the Church Security Program, now known as Welfare Services.

As secretary to the First Presidency I sat in most of the meetings pertaining to the organization of the welfare program, and was among the first to know of the call of the Pioneer Stake's young president to head the Churchwide program as its first managing director. For a quarter of a century President Lee served actively in the direction of this program. He can rightfully be recorded in Church history as the "father of the welfare program," though he would be the first to give others their full credit and recognize the sustaining powers and direction of the Almighty in formation of the vast program existing today throughout the Church.

True to his nature as a spiritual giant, with the overwhelming burden of responsibility for organizing the welfare program and implementing it squarely on his shoulders, President Lee turned first to the Lord for direction. On occasion he has related the following incident as an impressive spiritual experience:

I shall never forget April 20, 1935. I was a city commissioner in Salt Lake City. I was a stake president.

We had been wrestling with this question of welfare. There were few government work programs; the finances of the Church were low; we were told that there was not much that could be done so far as finances were concerned. And here we were with 4,800 of our 7,300 people who were wholly or partially dependent. We had only one place to go and that was to the Lord's program as set forth in the revelations.

It was from our humble efforts that the First Presidency, knowing that we had some experience, called me one morning, asking me if I would come to their office. It was Saturday morning; there were no appointments on their calendar, and for hours in that forenoon they talked with me and told me that they wanted me to resign from the city commission, and they would release me from being stake president; that they wished me now to head up the welfare movement to turn the tide from government relief, direct relief, and help to put the Church in a position where it could take care of its own needy.

After that morning I rode in my car (spring was just breaking) up to the head of City Creek Canyon, into what was then known as Rotary Park; and there, all by myself, I offered one of the most humble prayers of my life.

There I was, just a young man in my thirties. My experience had been limited. I was born in a little country town in Idaho. I had hardly been outside the boundaries of the states of Utah and Idaho. And now to put me in a position where I was to reach out to the entire membership of the Church, worldwide, was one of the most staggering contemplations that I could imagine. How could I do it with my limited understanding?

As I kneeled down, my petition was "What kind of an organiation should be set up in order to accomplish what the Presidency has assigned?" And there came to me on that glorious morning one of the most heavenly realizations of the power of the priesthood of God. It was as though something were saying in me, "There is no new organization necessary to take care of the needs of this people. All that is necessary is to put the priesthood of God to work. There is nothing else you need as a substitute."

As President Lee related this experience at a recent general priesthood meeting in the Tabernacle, to emphasize the applications of the priesthood, he made this additional comment:

With that understanding, then, and with the simple application of the power of the priesthood, the welfare program has gone forward now by leaps and bounds, overcoming obstacles that seemed impossible, until now it stands as a monument to the power of the priesthood, the like of which I could only glimpse in those days to which I have made reference.

That all was not easy in the task ahead, that there was rough sailing and obstacles, including opposition, to overcome, was indicated by President Lee a decade after this experience when, as a young apostle, he spoke of the welfare program during a series of weekly radio addresses. He said:

In harmony with that counsel [referring to Brigham Young's statement, "It is never any benefit to give out and out to man or woman, money, food, clothing or anything else, if they are able-bodied, and can work to earn what they need, when there is anything on earth for them to do,"] and obedient to the Lord's commandment, the Church in our day has developed a great movement known popularly or otherwise as the Church Welfare Program. Its purpose is to restore the unity, courage, faith and integrity of our pioneer fathers. We are like the ancient Israelites rebuilding the walls of our "fathers' sepulchres" that were broken down by the bondage of debt and public relief. In that task we have powerful aid from wonderful friends not members of the Church who have given us, as it were, "safe journey across their lands and permits to cut timber from the king's forests." Some of the governors of the land "were grieved when they heard that a man was come to seek the welfare of these modern children of Israel." The faithful among our membership have said, "Let us rise up and build and be independent from public gratitudes." So they strengthened their hands for the good work. We have had enemies who have scorned and ridiculed our efforts, and those who have argued that we ought to compromise our standards of independence. Others have resorted to threats of blackmail and still others have been hired to become traitors to their own people by the lure of worldly honors or public offices. These were the same methods of the enemy in the days of the Master when he was betrayed by his own people. They were likewise employed when the saints were driven from Nauvoo and when Johnston's Army came to Utah in 1857 because of false rumors that had been carried to the president of the United States by traitors and blackmailers. Success has always crowned the efforts of the children of the Lord whenever "the people had a mind to work." (*Youth and the Church,* 1970 ed., p. 204.)

As I relate these experiences and comments in the words of President Lee, I recall during the years that followed the many evidences that the First Presidency had full confidence in this young stake president whom they called upon to lead out in the welfare program. The First Presidency then consisted of President Heber J. Grant and his counselors, President J. Reuben Clark, Jr., and President David O. McKay. That their confidence was well placed and that successes followed the

devoted, courageous and energetic leadership of
this inspired man is evidenced not alone in the
solid foundation upon which the program now operates,
but also in the fact that six years later this same
Presidency called Harold B. Lee to fill a vacancy in
the Council of the Twelve, bringing him into the
position where he could rise to his present leadership of the Church.

I feel I would be correct if I made the assertion
that in yet another field of responsibility President
Lee has made another contribution to the Church
in every way as monumental as his welfare activities.
This has been in inspired leadership of the correlation
program of the past decade. Given assignment by
the First Presidency and especially inspired by President McKay, President Lee became the general chairman of the Church Correlation Committee. Again I
am certain that President Lee would want full credit to
be given to all others who assumed responsibilities, contributed ideas, and worked dilligently to bring success to
the program, but once again he arose to great heights
in fulfilling an assignment which came from the Lord
through inspired leaders.

The need for the program was fully impressed
upon President Lee, not only by the First Presidency,
but from his own observations and experiences in
the multiple assignments and responsibilities that
were his as a member of the Twelve.

Here again was an assignment which required
courage, practical wisdom, spiritual discernment.
It was no small task he and his committee confronted
in bringing into full correlation the vast curriculums,
programs, and objectives of the various priesthood
quorums and auxiliary organizations. The movement went forward to accomplish many changes
and achieve remarkable successes. I am sure it
was with deep satisfaction when, as president of

the Church, he was privileged a few months ago to announce what was probably the final major correlation step, and the one which he felt held promise of being the most far-reaching and important of the entire program. It was bringing the youth and young adult programs of the priesthood and Mutual Improvement Associations into full correlation. Thus, under his leadership, was created the Melchizedek Priesthood Mutual Interest Association and the Aaronic Priesthood Mutual Improvement Association. These programs are meeting with unusual success as they are now being implemented in the wards and stakes and missions and branches of the Church everywhere.

President Lee still retains a close association with the Church correlation program as a father watches over and rejoices in the successes of his offspring.

My position over the many years that President Lee has been an apostle has given me unquestioned assurance that he was and is a leader of great magnitude among his associates and is one to whom they long have looked for advice, counsel, and leadership.

His remarks at an M Men-Gleaner summer fireside in the Tabernacle on August 13, 1972, little more than a month after becoming president, manifest his wondersul spirit, his humility, and realization of the responsibilities that were his at this early date in his administration. I quote the following excerpts from his talk on that occasion:

Pray for me, young people. I plead with you to pray for me and I promise you that I will try to so live, that the Lord can answer your prayers through me. I'll try my best to be your servant.

The past few weeks have been overwhelming weeks of experience. A number who have interviewed me have said, "You are the head of the Church, aren't you?" I have answered, "No,

I'm not the head of the Church. The Lord and Savior, Jesus Christ, is the head of this church. I happen to be the one who has been called to preside over his church at the present time here upon the earth."

The true Church is the most powerful weapon against evil philosophies and false ideas, President Lee explained to the young people. "There is no more powerful weapon that can be forged than the powerful teaching of the gospel of Jesus Christ."

Always a powerful champion for righteousness, President Lee also said on that occasion:

There are two things that, when fully applied, would save .the world. The first is to put the full might of the priesthood of the kingdom of God to work, and the second is the powerful teachings of the gospel of Jesus Christ.

No truly converted Latter-day Saint can be dishonest, or lie, or steal. That means that one may have a testimony as of today, but when he stoops to do things that contradict the laws of God, it is because he has lost his testimony and he has to fight to regain it. Testimony is not something that you have today and you keep always. Testimony is either going to grow to a brightness of certainty, or it is going to diminish to nothingness, depending on what we do about it. The testimony that we recapture day by day is the thing that saves us from pitfalls of the adversary. . . .

The Lord is nearer to us than we have any idea. Keep in mind that the Holy Ghost is one of the Godhead. The Lord said about his nearness: "Draw near unto me and I will draw near unto you; seek me diligently and ye shall find me, ask and ye shall receive, knock and it shall be opened unto you." Now this means that the Lord is not keeping himself away from us; it is we who keep ourselves away from him.

As Latter-day Saints we should be aware of and always keep in mind the instructions given by the Lord relative to the president of the Church, whoever he may be, as contained in section 21 of the Doctrine and Covenants. These are the words of the revelation given to the Prophet Joseph Smith on the day the Church was organized, April 6, 1830:

Behold there shall be a record kept among you, and in it thou shalt be called a seer, a translator, a prophet, an apostle of Jesus Christ, an elder of the Church through the will of the Father, and the grace of your Lord, Jesus Christ.

Being inspired of the Holy Ghost to lay the foundation thereof, and to build it up unto the most holy faith.

Which Church was organized and established in the year of your Lord eighteen hundred and thirty, in the fourth month, and on the sixth day of the month, which is called April.

Wherefore, meaning the Church, thou shalt give heed unto all his words and commandments which he shall give unto you as he receiveth them and walking in holiness before me:

For his word ye shall receive, as if from mine own mouth, in all patience and faith;

For by doing these things the gates of hell shall not prevail against you; yea, and the Lord God will disperse the powers of darkness from before you, and cause the heavens to shake for your good, and his name's glory.

President Lee seeks always to walk by the Spirit. He lives in thought and deed to be worthy of the manifestations of the Spirit of the Lord, and that they come and he is receptive is evident on all sides. As an example, I cite from the account President Lee wrote recently of his visit to the Holy Land, including Jerusalem. He wrote, at the beginning of the article printed in the *Ensign* in April 1972:

As we approached the Holy Land we read together the harmony of the four gospel narratives so beautifully put together President J. Reuben Clark, Jr., and then as we left our room each time, we prayed that the Lord would deafen our ears to what the guide said about historical places but would make us keenly sensitive to the spiritual feeling so that we would know by impression, rather than hearing, where the sacred spots were.

Then President Lee recounted some of his choice spiritual impressions, wherein in some places, "we felt none of the spiritual significance that we felt at other places."

I came away from some of these experiences never to feel the same again about the mission of our Lord and Savior. I had impressed upon me, as I have never had it impressed before, what it means to be a special witness. I say with all the conviction of my soul, I know that Jesus lives. I know that he was the very Son of God. And I know that in this church and in the gospel of Jesus Christ is to be found the way to salvation.

The Lord has called Harold B. Lee to lead the Church at this time, and he is the representative of the Lord, and I testify that he is entitled to and does receive revelation from God for the blessing and guidance of this people. He has but one thought and that is to know the mind and will of the Lord and to convey it to the Latter-day Saints. He is just as much a prophet of God as were his predecessors. Let us be submissive to counsel and advice from him whom the Lord has thus appointed. Strong men in the past, who have even stood in the presence of the Lord, have apostatized from this church because they were not willing to follow the living oracles, the leadership of the Church.

This is indeed a time when the Church and the world need strong and inspired leadership. President Lee is the man who is fully capable of and does provide that leadership. He is in very deed and by divine right the man of the hour.

9

Counselors to President Lee

I am certain that all of the General Authorities of the Church, with whom I am now numbered, as well as the membership of the Church generally were universally highly thrilled with the two counselors chosen by President Harold B. Lee.

Even though the appointments were not really unexpected, yet I feel I know President Lee well enough to be sure that he would not make such an important decision without knowing the mind and will of the Lord in the matter. It is satisfying to know that both President N. Eldon Tanner and President Marion G. Romney were so favored of the Lord that one would be invited to continue his faithful service in the First Presidency and that the other had so magnified himself in his apostolic calling that he could be summoned to higher responsibilities.

President Lee became the eleventh president of the Church on Friday, July 7, 1972, just a few days following the death of President Joseph Fielding Smith, whom he had served faithfully and loyally as a counselor for two and one-half years.

President Tanner had served along with President Lee as second counselor to President Smith, which position he also held with President McKay. He had so proven himself and his capabilities had been recognized by President Lee to the degree that he was appointed first counselor.

All of us had known of the long friendship and
close association of President Lee with Elder Romney
and of the remarkable parallel in their service to the
Church. Their close association began when they were
both named General Authorities the same day in
April 1941. At that annual conference President Lee,
who had been serving for several years as the managing director of the welfare program, was named to fill
the vacancy in the Council of the Twelve occasioned
by the death of Elder Melvin J. Ballard, a much-loved
apostle.

That conference also saw the appointment of the
first five Assistants to the Council of the Twelve,
who are designated as "High Priests and Assistants
to the Twelve." Elder Romney, then presiding over
the Bonneville Stake, was the first of the five so
named. The others were Elders Thomas E. McKay,
Clifford E. Young, Alma Sonne, and Nicholas G.
Smith.

It was in June of that year that Elder Romney was
appointed as assistant managing director of the welfare program, and thus began the closest of associations between President Lee and President Romney
as they united in a service to their fellowmen through
this divine program, which lasted well beyond a score
of years. President Lee had the privilege ten years
later to welcome his close associate into the ranks
of the Twelve Apostles, and together they have shared
assignments and responsibilities in directing the
priesthood and carrying forward the extensive and
somewhat revolutionary program of Church
correlation.

The three—President Lee, President Tanner, and
President Romney—make as strong a First Presidency
as any I have been privileged to associate with. There
is among them a unity of purpose, a strength of leadership, and an inspired vision of the role of the Church
as it expands worldwide. Theirs is a virile leader-

ship with a dedication and devotion to highest purposes that is contagious throughout the Church. Under their inspired leadership the Church will move steadily forward in its accomplishments of the Lord's purposes.

I love these brethren and fully accept them as the Lord's anointed. To me they are in every way worthy of their high office, and I sustain them as prophets, seers, and revelators.

PRESIDENT MARION G. ROMNEY

Of all the brethren who have become members of the First Presidency since I entered my service in President Grant's office 50 years ago, there is none with whom I was better acquainted personally before the call to such high office came than Marion G. Romney.

President Marion G. Romney was the author's former bishop and stake president before becoming a General Authority in 1941.

One of the greatest blessings the Lord has granted me is the friendship of good and noble men. Each one has greatly influenced my life for good, not only because of what he has said or done or achieved, but because of what he is personally, his personal radiation. For years before he became a General Authority in 1941, I felt highly honored to count President Romney as one of my very dear friends. He had been first my bishop and then my stake president.

I have most sincerely admired him over the years as I have seen his devotion and growth in the Church as a leader and exemplar. He has grown in eminence in the Church day by day. Like so many others who have risen to such prominence in the Church, his beginnings in life were of a humble nature. He has reached prominence in his chosen law profession and in his church service largely through his own determination and strong desires to succeed. From his sturdy faithful parents and grandparents, who were among the pioneers to the Salt Lake Valley, he inherited not wealth and affluence, but love for his fellowmen, faith in God, the value of determined struggle and hard work even for his very existence, and a desire to know and achieve the true purposes of life. He was not unacquainted with hardship and some privation in his youthful years.

Marion G. Romney was born of American parentage in Mexico toward the end of the last century—September 1897, in Colonia Juarez, one of the Mormon colonies. His parents had gone to the Mexican colonies in 1885 when they and other Latter-day Saint families received permission from that government to settle in northern Mexico.

The youths who grew up in those Mexican colonies were well trained and highly disciplined in the ways of the gospel. They came from rugged stock, characterized by deep faith and a will to win in the battle of life against sometimes seemingly insurmountable odds. They were honest and independent, and their concern about the temporal and spiritual welfare of those about them built a strong spirit of brotherhood.

Out of this atmosphere came Marion G. Romney, while only a youth in his teens, yet entrusted with the responsibilities and work of a man. His family members were forced from Mexico during the exodus, and the father, George S. Romney, entrusted his 15-year-old eldest son, Marion, with the task of caring for the family during the trek northward, while the men of the colonies remained behind to look after as best they could their property and bring out as many cattle as possible.

President Romney has often told the story that when his family came out of Mexico, the wagon contained as provisions mostly sacks of beans. He explained that they had beans for breakfast and lunch, and dinner, and his mother knew as many ways to cook beans as anyone. As he grew to manhood, he was accustomed to privation and the necessity to work hard to eke out an existence.

After attending schools in Mexico and in Idaho, where his family eventually settled, President Romney had a strong desire to go on a mission. He had been working and had saved some money, and when he approached his father on the matter, it seemed even then an impossible achievement. He told his father that he had saved some money and asked if the father would go with him to the bank and sign a note for enough money for the mission. This was done, and the call came to go to the Australian Mission. When he returned from his mission, he obtained employment and repaid the loan.

It was this same independent spirit that helped him to provide for a family and at the same time gain an education and win a law degree. For a dozen years President Romney practiced law in Salt Lake City, holding prominent positions, and also served as a member of the legislature. His was a constant quest for knowledge, and with that knowledge came wisdom and understanding.

He was not left alone to achieve learning and wisdom. A grandfather, who was a patriarch, had laid his hands on Marion's head before he had reached his twelfth birthday. From this blessing, the young lad knew that if he remained worthy of it and met the requirements, he would have the Spirit and power of the Lord ever to be his guide. He was warned that if he was to achieve his desire to perform a great and mighty work, there was necessity to seek wisdom in the morning of his life. This has always been President Romney's goal—to achieve wisdom through his studies, through the experiences of life, and through knowing the word of the Lord and seeking his guiding hand.

One of his favorite and oft-repeated passages of scripture is found in the Book of Mormon and contains the instructions of the prophet Alma to his son, Helaman:

O, remember, my son, and learn wisdom in thy youth; yea, learn in thy youth to keep the commandments of God.

Yea, and cry unto God for all thy support; yea, let all thy doings be unto the Lord, and whithersoever thou goest let it be in the Lord; yea, let thy thoughts be directed unto the Lord; yea, let the affections of thy heart be placed upon the Lord forever.

Counsel with the Lord in all thy doings, and he will direct thee for good; yea, when thou liest down at night lie down unto the Lord, that he may watch over you in your sleep; and when thou risest in the morning let thy heart be full of thanks unto God; and if ye do these things ye shall be lifted up at the last day. (Alma 37:35-37.)

Not only has President Romney preached sermons on this theme over the pulpit, but there have been many silent sermons, more impressive, more effectively taught by the example of his life. I have never known a man who was more spiritual than President Romney, nor one who lived closer to the Lord.

His prayers are always impressive. He approaches the Lord in full faith, with sincerity and a humility that testifies that here is one man who knows the Lord and that He directs the lives of men who faithfully serve him. There is always a warmth and earnestness about his prayers as if he is speaking directly to his Father in heaven and knows that the words coming from his heart are being heard.

Another outstanding quality of President Romney that has always impressed me so much is his thorough knowledge of the gospel, of the holy scriptures, and his ability to preach sincerely and interpret the word of the Lord. His brethren always listen intently and respectfully when he speaks of the doctrines of the kingdom.

Significant in his discussions of the gospel and of the problems and challenges facing the Church today is his keen intellect, his ability to analyze situations and present his decisions and conclusions with a clarity of thought that reveals a profound wisdom and understanding that must be heaven-inspired. Such knowledge can only be acquired by constant study and prayerful contemplation, both of which are integral parts of his own life. His sermons are given in a calm, deliberate, and contemplative manner, and on occasion it has been with great emotion that he has borne his sure witness of the divinity of the Lord and Savior Jesus Christ. There is never any question about the certainty of that testimony as it touches the hearts of his listeners.

I was inspired as I read recently in the *Ensign* a few quotations from President Romney's patriarchal blessings. They were in an article on his life by his beloved associate, President Spencer W. Kimball of the Council of the Twelve. Because they so effectively portray the man I know President Romney to be, I include the quotation from the blessing and the few words of comment by President Kimball that immediately followed. President Romney was told:

You will be held in high honor and respected by the people, beyond your comprehension; your counsel will be sought; your posterity will honor you; your faith will carry you through. Thy faith shall unfold to you the mysteries of the Kingdom, and things which are not understood or comprehended by people shall be made plain to you. Visions of the future shall be opened unto your mind and you shall see the handiwork of the Lord in all things, for faith similar to that enjoyed by the Brother of Jared shall be yours to enjoy. . . . Thou shalt be called to labor further in positions of trust and leadership in the interest of the Lord's work.

Then commented President Kimball:

To those of us who have known President Romney long and intimately, we have seen these long-promised blessings in fruition and have come to realize that the making of a Marion G. Romney was not the work of a few decades, but has been an eternal thing bringing together all the great qualifications and opportunities and tests, privileges, challenges, and times into a whole to prepare this great soul for the opportunities he now has. The name of Christ and his gospel is not merely mentioned but is ploughed deep in his consciousness.

Oh, how my heart echoes response to the words of this blessing and President Kimball's comments. I know them to be true.

I have previously commented elsewhere in this book on President Romney's long association with President Lee and President Moyle in launching and perfecting the great welfare program. It is not necessary to repeat, but only to say that he devoted many years of his time to this program, in which service he has visited most of the stakes and missions. He shall always be remembered for his untiring efforts and unlimited energy in carrying this message throughout the Church.

He is a builder. He learned the carpenter trade when a young man, and I can remember when he built his own home in Salt Lake City. But he has been primarily a builder of souls and has had an influence in building character and faith in thousands of people with whom he has come in contact in his positions of leadership and as a humble servant of the Master.

In his various appointments of leadership he has taken deep satisfaction in the opportunities that have come to him to forward the destiny of the Church. He is a man of great inspiration, and the Lord has magnified him in a marvelous way. To me it seems

only natural and proper that President Lee, through
the inspiration of the Lord, should call Marion G.
Romney to be one of his counselors in the First
Presidency.

From my own experience and association with the
brethren over the years I have recognized that President Romney has had the love and confidence of his
associates as they have called upon him with assurance to carry the torch in many responsibilities
pertaining to the work of the Lord. Along with his
many other characteristics, he has a remarkable
sense of honor. He is approachable and inspires confidence and love. It has always been a joy to be in his
company to partake of his counsel, his humor, his
wisdom and inspiration. He loves the people of the
Church. He understands the divine principle of the
brotherhood of man. He understands the purpose of
life and devotes himself unselfishly to the service of
others and is untiring in his efforts to share the gospel with others. The missionary program, worldwide,
has felt his influence, especially in areas to which he
has been assigned supervision.

He, like his beloved associates, understands and
proclaims throughout the world the divine mission of
our Lord and Savior, which is to assist in bringing to
pass the immortality and eternal life of man in the
celestial kingdom of our Heavenly Father. Their mission is to all mankind.

SECTION SIX

In Retrospect

Pictures of the author, Joseph Anderson, at various times during his long career of Church service.

10

Church Growth and the Passing of Time

Perhaps nowhere else does one recognize the changes wrought by the passing of time more than at the Church offices, especially when one spends so many years working with the brethren of the General Authorities. Men who were young when I commenced working there have become old with the passing of years and others who were older—and some who were not so old—have passed on, while others have taken their places. With these changes have come changes in methods also.

Of course, one cannot fail to recognize also that the years are making an indelible impression upon himself, and that while he is not advancing in seniority so far as quorum position is concerned, he too is changing with the passing of the years.

The Church never stands still, nor does it move backward at any time. It marches steadily on under the inspiration of the Lord, who is the author of our salvation and whose church it is. Fifty years ago there were about 89 or 90 stakes, whereas today, at the time of this writing, there are more than 600.

Fifty years ago two of us as secretaries—Sister

Bertha Irvine and I—could take care of the clerical
work for the First Presidency. Now it requires nine or
ten secretaries and stenographers to serve in this
capacity. A similar—in fact, a much greater—change
has taken place in the finance, accounting, and other
departments of the First Presidency's office, and the
same is true of other departments.

Whereas years ago the branches in many missions
particularly had to be satisfied to hold their meetings
in lodge halls and other rented quarters, now the
mission branches throughout the world are fast building
their own edifices. Wards are multiplying so rapidly
that buildings cannot be erected fast enough to ac-
commodate them.

The faith and devotion of the people also are in-
creasing. Some years ago about 15 to 20 percent of
the members attended their sacrament meetings. Today
the average is more than 38 percent. The same significant and commendable change has taken place in other
areas of church activity, such as tithe-paying, ward
teaching (now called home teaching), youth programs,
priesthood activities, etc.

The Church has grown in numbers from 560,696
in 1922 to 3,217,790 at the close of 1972.

Divine Guidance

I have been thrilled and my faith greatly strengthened as I have had opportunity and occasion to read
the records of the past, dating back to the time of
Brigham Young, and to learn that the same divine
spirit of inspiration and revelation is guiding the leaders
of today that guided those of former times. The
Church has not found it necessary at any time to say,
"We made a mistake in those days and have learned
better since." It is true that it has become necessary to
discontinue, for the time being at least, certain practices
—not because a mistake was made, but because people

and laws made it necessary to do so; but the fundamentals of the gospel have never changed.

Verily, verily, I say unto you, that when I give a commandment to any of the sons of men to do a work unto my name, and those sons of men go with all their might and with all they have to perform that work, and cease not their diligence, and their enemies come upon them and hinder them from performing that work, behold, it behooveth me to require that work no more at the hands of those sons of men, but to accept of their offerings.

And the iniquity and transgression of my holy laws and commandments I will visit upon the heads of those who hindered my work, unto the third and fourth generation, so long as they repent not, and hate me, saith the Lord God.

Therefore, for this cause have I accepted the offerings of those whom I commanded to build up a city and a house unto my name, in Jackson County, Missouri, and were hindered by their enemies, saith the Lord your God.

And I will answer judgment, wrath, and indignation, wailing, and anguish, and gnashing of teeth upon their heads, unto the third and fourth generation, so long as they repent not, and hate me, saith the Lord your God.

And this I make an example unto you, for your consolation concerning all those who have been commanded to do a work and have been hindered by the hands of their enemies, and by oppression, saith the Lord your God. (D&C 124:49-53.)

I have found the Church to be the greatest service organization in the world. It has no selfish purposes. It has, however, fabulous rewards to offer to those who accept its divine teachings and live in accordance therewith, the ultimate reward being eternal life in the kingdom of our Heavenly Father. The reward of righteous living, in accordance with God's eternal plan, is not confined to the hereafter, for no man can follow the inspired teachings revealed for his guidance without obtaining a richer and happier life than one who fails to take advantage of these things.

The Lord has said, "This is my work and my glory—to bring to pass the immortality and eternal life of man." Our Savior laid down his life that this might be accomplished, and he also gave us the plan

whereby we can individually achieve this goal. It is the
mission of the Church to serve as the vehicle by which
this great work can be accomplished. From the very
beginning of this dispensation men have been called
and set apart by our Father's representatives here on
earth to carry the glad tidings of great joy, the plan
of life and salvation, to our Father's children wherever
they can be reached. Sometimes men are called upon
to make what appear to be sacrifices in order to serve
as missionaries of the truth or to preside over missions
in various parts of the world. However, no one who
has given his life for this cause—devoting himself
unselfishly and sincerely thereto—has failed to reap
rewards that cannot be measured in dollars and cents.
Money cannot buy salvation, but the true treasures
are those which are laid up in heaven, where moth
and rust do not currupt nor thieves break through and
steal.

The brethren who stand at the head of the Church
give unstintingly and unselfishly of their time and their
talents, under the inspiration of the Lord, for the
advancement of his kingdom upon the earth and for
the blessing of others. Sometimes it would seem that
they give of their strength to such an extent as might
seem unwise so far as proper concern for their health
would suggest. However, it is almost the general feeling
among them that the work is so important and so urgent
that they will serve with all their heart, might, mind,
and strength so long as life permits, they being fully
assured that they are engaged in the work of the Lord.

Observations Regarding Prayer

I am convinced that one can obtain a proper opinion of a person's character, and especially of his faith
and sincerity, by listening to him pray. I am sure that
no people pray more earnestly and more frequently than
do the Latter-day Saints. As is undoubtedly the case

with all religious people, our little children learn to call upon their Heavenly Father on bended knees and otherwise and are encouraged to take their turn in family prayer. I appreciate that it is not the words that are spoken, although the words betray the feelings of the heart, but it is the faith and sincerity that the Lord recognizes.

President Grant occasionally told of his experience as a child, living as he did just across the street from Brigham Young. Upon hearing the bell calling Brigham Young's family to prayer, he would run across the street, enter the president's home, and kneel with the family in their evening devotion. He has also told us that Brother Brigham talked to the Lord as though he were present, and that he, the boy, at times opened his eyes, expecting to see the Lord standing there.

Amulek, a brother of Alma, said regarding prayer:

Cry unto him when ye are in your fields, yea, over all your flocks.

Cry unto him in your houses, yea, over all your household, both morning, mid-day and evening.

Yea, cry unto him against the power of your enemies.

Yea, cry unto him against the evil one, who is an enemy to all righteousness.

Cry unto him over the crops of your field, that ye may prosper in them.

Cry over the flocks of your fields, that they may increase.

But this is not all; ye must pour out your souls in your closets, and your secret places, and in your wilderness.

Yea, and when you do not cry unto the Lord, let your hearts be full, drawn out in prayer unto him continually for your welfare, and also for the welfare of those who are around you. (Alma 34:20-27.)

It has been my good fortune to be with the brethren of the General Authorities when they have prayed while traveling with them, on trains, in hotel rooms, in the homes of the Saints, in meetings, and wherever we have been together. I have heard them express their innermost desires and gratitude to our Heavenly Father, and I have joined in their prayers and taken my turn with them. No one can tell me these humble prayers were not from the heart and that they did not ascend to the throne of our divine Father.

On literally thousands of occasions I have heard the brethren pray in council meetings, particularly in the temple, as on bended knees they have pleaded with the Lord for his blessings, and again as they have surrounded the holy altar. Those prayers have not been mere words, but humble petitions for our Father's blessings and guidance, and they have been answered in blessings upon the people individually and collectively and upon the Church. The spirit of prayer has been evidenced and the presence of our Lord has been recognized, although perhaps not visible.

I question that one can approach nearer to the throne of grace and feel more vividly the influence of the Holy Spirit than in the meetings of the First Presidency and the Twelve in the temple of the Lord. This is particularly true when these brethren are engaged in calling upon our Father, expressing gratitude for his blessings and humbly and sincerely appealing for his help and guidance. The power of the priesthood is manifest; God's highest authority upon earth is there present. As the servants of the Lord, they humble themselves before him, testifying in prayer of his goodness to them, pleading for his inspiration to assist them in their labors, and beseeching his blessings upon the Church, the world, and his children generally.

Such prayers include sincere expressions of gratitude for the gospel and for the Lord's blessings unto his servants. They plead for inspiration to attend each of them as they fulfill the duties assigned to them and appear before the people to give them the word of the Lord. They ask that the General Authorities as well as stake, ward, and quorum authorities set proper examples, not only before the members of the Church, but also before the people of the world. They seek aid for the missionaries and officers in organized wards and branches, that they may be led to the honest investigators and that the influence of Christ's church may be spread throughout the world for good. They pray for the whisperings of the Holy Spirit and the revelations of the Lord's mind and will, and for help so to live hourly and daily, constantly, that they may merit the Lord's guidance and be responsive to his inspiration and voice.

They pray for the priesthood everywhere, for men who hold it and are somewhat indifferent, that they may realize what it means to hold the priesthood, to be the Lord's representative in the assignments that may be given to them.

They call for blessings upon the president of the United States, his cabinet, the Congress and the judiciary, and all who hold government office; that the Lord will frustrate the plans of the enemy of freedom, and particularly those who are opposed to the gospel of Jesus Christ; that the influence of truth and righteousness may be strengthened.

Remembered always are the down-hearted and sad, that their worthiness may be increased, that they may receive the guidance and blessing of our Heavenly Father.

They pray for the sick—those who are suffering and distressed; for the world, that war might be averted, if it is in harmony with the purpose of the Lord; that people may trust one another more than they have heretofore done, and eventually accept those principles which will bring peace on earth and goodwill toward men.

They plead for strength to live in such a way that they may never be left a moment without the guiding and prompting influence of our Heavenly Father.

In their prayers they make covenant with the Lord that they will keep his commandments and that they

will do their duty daily in order that they may gain
strength and thus become worthy of the Lord's blessing
and guidance.

His Servants Magnified

It has always been an added source of testimony to
me to witness the growth, spiritual and mental, of men
who have been called to positions of authority in the
Church, particularly men who have been selected to fill
vacancies in the councils of the General Authorities.

On one occasion, after President Heber J. Grant
had delivered an address on the sugar beet industry
before the National Chemurgic Conference in Detroit,
Michigan, I expressed to him my astonishment that his
address had received such a great ovation from those
present, they being among the oustanding scientists,
educators, and industrialists of the nation. The remarks
of no one of all the other speakers had received the
reception that President Grant's had received, and he
was the only one who was invited to speak a second
time at this conference, the second occasion being the
banquet given the guests the following evening.

In answer to my comment on the subject, President
Grant made the remark, the truth of which I have
subsequently recognized perhaps more than I had
theretofore done, "Joseph, one of the great testimonies
of the truth of this work is that the Lord magnifies his
servants."

As men have been called through the inspiration of
the Lord to positions of responsibility in this church, if
they have magnified their callings and subjected themselves to the guidance of the Spirit of the Lord—and it
has been my experience that this has generally been the
case—it is my testimony that they have grown in spiritual
and mental stature in a remarkable way, in a miraculous
way, in a manner far beyond the possibilities of human
attainment.

These men have never become commonplace to

me—I have never looked upon them as merely remarkable men. To me they have always been servants of the living God, honored by him; and the Twelve are special witnesses of the Lord Jesus Christ. It has been my great fortune and privilege to be as near to them—if not more so—as other men, and yet I have never looked upon them with anything other than a spirit of reverence and love. I have not found among them any that I have not loved and admired. I testify to these things because I know from my experience with these men that such conditions just could not be if the Church were false or were merely a sect or denomination led by men of good intentions but not recognized of the Lord. Our Master, the Redeemer and Savior of mankind, is our leader. It is his church, and his inspiration and revelation that guide and direct those who have been called to represent him. And yet, with it all, they are human and subject to human frailties.

Each one has made his individual impression for good upon my life, and each has been very different from the others. No two of these brethren have been alike. As a matter of fact, no two individuals are alike. The Lord in his great wisdom has prepared these men for the service they have performed and are rendering. I am satisfied that their training is not limited to this world, but that they were selected and ordained before they came here for the work they were to perform.

In my discussion of these brethren, I have selected only a certain few whose lives and service are merely illustrative of all who have been called to serve as special witnesses of the Lord in this day and age. The Lord has magnified them and blessed them with special talents and abilities for the particular time in which they served, and he has inspired them by his Holy Spirit. I have found them different in a sense from other men—they have a keen sense of duty, and they are attended by a spirit superior to that which other men possess.

Notwithstanding my nearness to them over the years

and their expressed confidence in and love for me, they
never impress me as being other than special servants
of the Lord, inspired by him, and men who carry with
them an influence and power peculiar to their high
callings. I have- never felt inclined to speak lightly or
unkindly of any one of these men, recognizing as I do
that the Lord has honored them with this special
calling. To me they are apostles of the Lord and have
the same power and authority as did the apostles of
the Master in the meridian of time. Then too, each is a
potential president of the Church, the mouthpiece of the
Lord to this people. Experience has definitely indicated
to me time and time again that they are prophets of
the Lord and that they serve under his inspiration and
guidance in the work they are called upon to do, in
choosing men to preside over stakes, in selecting
patriarchs, in pronouncing blessings when setting
apart men and women for general positions and also
for positions of responsibility and leadership in stakes,
wards, and missions, and in all other activities.

Consideration for the Repentant Transgressor

It has been my experience that the brethren of the
General Authorities are men of judgment, or discretion,
and of compassionate consideration. These men—and
I speak particularly of the brethren of the First Presidency—are not fanatical or narrow-minded; they have
perhaps more concern and consideration for the sinner,
if he shows a disposition to repent—and they are
always anxious that he does repent—than have the
great majority of the members of the Church. Like the
Savior, they are not inclined to condemn harshly those
who have made mistakes and show by their conduct
that they have sincerely repented. They have a love for
mankind, and would that all might hear and accept the
truth and thus obtain the joy that comes into the hearts
of faithful Latter-day Saints in the knowledge of the
truth of the restored gospel of Chirst.

As President Brigham Young once said, they recognize that the gospel is merely the truth—

—That it includes all truth wherever found, in all the words of God and man, and that man to be truly educated must know of things on the earth, above the earth, and under the earth; that all men are subject to error and have ample room for improvement; that one of the great principles of the Gospel is repentance; that we are all our Heavenly Father's children; and that he is pleased when his erring children turn from their evil ways and seek to serve him. We are all as little children in a certain sense, and we grow by overcoming, by humbling ourselves before the Lord, acknowledging our faults to him and to his chosen representatives, turning away from sin, thus learning the true secret of growth by attempting to live in accordance with the true and high principles of joy and happiness that our Father has given us in his glorious Gospel.

These principles were so beautifully exemplified in the life and teachings of President George Albert Smith, who sincerely looked upon all mankind as "our Father's children"—members of the Church and nonmembers alike—and who so generously and wholeheartedly sought to help people of every faith and of no faith with whom he came in contact, to improve their lives, that they might be made partakers of the blessings that our Heavenly Father has vouchsafed unto all who will render obedience to him.

The words of Nephi in the fourth chapter of Second Nephi in the Book of Mormon have had an influence on my life, and I know the thoughts therein expressed are true: "Yea, I know that God will give liberally to him that asketh. Yea, God will give me if I ask not amiss."

I thank the Lord for faith; and like Nephi of old, I know that the Lord will give me if I do not ask amiss.

Repentance

I have learned over the years that the great Scottish poet Robert Burns understood human nature well when he said, "Man's inhumanity to man makes countless millions mourn." On the other hand, man's kindness to man, especially when it comes from the heart, brings happiness to the soul of many a disheartened and discouraged individual. It is deeply regrettable that everyone cannot learn and put into practice the teachings of the Master that we should love our neighbor as ourselves.

Experience has demonstrated very clearly and definitely that the secret to happiness lies in service to others, in kindness and love extended to others, and especially to those who are in distress, discouraged, and disheartened, whether that condition is brought about by sin or by misfortune. My soul has often been made to rejoice and I have seen people touched by the spirit of kindness and forgiveness extended by the brethren to whom they have brought their problems.

On the other hand, it has also been necessary that the requirements of justice should be measured out to those who have fallen from the path of rectitude, in their own interests as well as the interest of the Church. It is always easier to grant than refuse the appeal for forgiveness of the individual who has transgressed when that pleading comes with tears. It requires a firm determination and the guidance of the Holy Spirit to insist upon justice rather than undue mercy. Justice must have its rightful portion also if the scales are to be fairly balanced, even though at times unhappiness, sorrow, and remorse must punish the transgressor. One gains strength to overcome evil and to live righteously by forsaking his evil tendencies, and if after being forgiven he resorts to his former impure practices, his condition is not improved but made worse. The Lord has said: "By this ye may know that a man has forsaken his sins, behold he will confess and forsake them."

Forsaking is an important element in repentance and generally requires a period of some considerable time to make sure that the individual can live righteously thereafter, notwithstanding he may feel in his heart that he has fully repented.

When one has truly overcome his transgression and has proven his ability to live righteously in the future, joy and happiness come into the soul and a peace that passeth understanding. Repentance, of course, is far more than sorrow for the sin, although that is a necessary element. One must do all in his power to make amends for the wrong he has done and manifest by a righteous life that he has truly forsaken his sin.

One principle that has made an indelible impression upon me, and one that I too have striven to exemplify in my life, is that we should not form opinions blindly nor should we find fault with our fellowmen, but should always seek for the good in one another. My brethren have taught me well that man is God's greatest creation, and it should be our constant endeavor to improve ourselves, that our own lives may be a light to others and that by following that light, they may be led to glorify our Father who is in heaven.

Employees

No treatise of this kind would be complete without a reference to my fellow employees. These men and women have partaken of the spirit of the brethren of the authorities, and those whom I have known intimately over the years were and are as noble and fine as human beings can be. I shall mention only a very few who have passed from this life. An entire volume could be written about these faithful people, those now living and those who have gone to their reward.

Outstanding in my memory is Arthur Winter, who, while not carrying the title, was financial secretary, or treasurer, of the Church. He had commenced his services in the Church offices when a very young man, having come here as an immigrant boy from England. There just are no better men, in my judgment, than was

Arthur Winter—a man of great wisdom and ability whom the First Presidency trusted implicitly, and who never betrayed that trust in the slightest. If when I pass on I can have the friendship and association of Arthur Winter and men like him, I shall feel that I have not lived in vain. He did not aspire to position, he did not seek the plaudits of men, but in my judgment he was worthy of the association of our Father's choicest servants, and I am sure he has earned the encomium of his Lord, "Well done, good and faithful servant; enter thou into the joy of thy Lord."

Space will not permit mentioning all of the wonderful persons with whom I have served over the years. They are many. I cannot, however, fail to mention Bertha Irvine, with whom I worked so many years, and who commenced working for the First Presidency in the days of President Wilford Woodruff. She performed an outstanding service to the brethren. She gave me every consideration when as a young man I became the president's secretary and secretary to the First Presidency. We worked together over the years.

Sister Agnes Rutherford, an old Scottish lady who dusted the First Presidency's offices, was a humble, sweet, and high-class lady. She loved to be in the offices of the Church leadership and to counsel with the office help. I am not prepared to say what her reward in the hereafter will be, but I am assured in my own thinking that wherever she is she will be thinking of and trying to help others. Her kindly solicitude and friendliness were worthy of a true Saint, and I am certain the Lord will reward her accordingly.

Henry O'Gorman spent several years as guide in the Church Office Building. He was a genuine English gentlemen who had been assistant postmaster in Liverpool before coming to Utah. Sweet memories crowd upon me as I think of that wonderful gentleman, for gentleman and Saint he was in the truest sense. Seldom, if ever, did a morning pass that Brother O'Gorman did not come into my office, shake hands with me, and express his love for me. When I asked him how he was, his ready answer was, "If I can only be faithful to the end!" I often remarked, "Brother O'Gorman, there should be no question in your mind on that score." He would reply, "One never knows." Needless to say, Brother O'Gorman did prove faithful to the end, and the Lord made known to him when his passing was to be, and he was prepared to go and welcomed the call when it came.

Carl A. Carlson was employed in the accounting department and served the Church for over 50 years. When I commenced working for the president, I frequently had some spare time, which I occupied working on the general books of the Church, assisting Brother Carlson. No man could have been kinder to me. My slightest desire was quickly fulfilled by him in the matter of office supplies, equipment, or whatever it might be. He loved the brethren, and his greatest joy was in serving them.

I cannot say that I have known a man who lived a perfect life. If I have known such, I am unaware of it, and if there be or has been such a person, save only the Savior of the world, he, I am sure, would be the last to make any such claim; for were he to do so, it would be but an indication of imperfection.

11

What a Wonderful Work!

The strong testimonies borne by the brethren over the years impress me with the fact that it is not possible for us to pay enough attention to the importance of having an individual testimony of the gospel. Every Latter-day Saint needs to know for himself that this is the work of the Lord, and that this is the only true church of Christ. Yes, other churches have much truth and much that is good, and I am sure many are doing a great work as far as they go. But there is only one true church that is recognized of God as his church. Everyone should know, as I know with all my heart and soul, that the Lord has conferred his divine authority upon men in our day.

What a wonderful work this is when we analyze it—that we have the authority from God to act in his name, that we have the authority in his church to seal on earth and it will be sealed in heaven. No other church claims that authority. We have the responsibility and the authority of doing the work for our kindred dead, that they too may enjoy the blessings of eternal life. There is nothing selfish about the nature of work in this church. We are not working "just for me and my wife and my son John." We are working for them and all our ancestral dead—yea—but we are working also for all of our Father's children.

". . . this is my work and my glory—to bring to pass the immortality and eternal life of man," all men—and this is our work and glory too, I am sure.

As a church we seem to have reached a point where we do not have the severe persecution we once had, but that does not mean that the evil one is not alert. He may not use the same tactics, but one of the most difficult trials we have to face is prosperity. We must have a testimony of the truth of the gospel. We must live near to the Lord if we expect to have his favor, if we expect to obtain his blessings. We must have in our hearts a knowledge of the truth of this work. The Lord said that he who heard his sayings and complied with them was like the wise man who built his house upon a rock.

The great commandment is that we shall love God, and the second is like unto it, that we shall love our neighbor as ourselves. If the love of God has taken root in our hearts, and if we are demonstrating that love in our lives, it will bear fruit and will cause us to come to a knowledge of God, whom to know is life eternal.

There are many people who profess to believe in Christ, the Redeemer of the world, who do not believe in that vital principle of the gospel, the principle by which Peter knew that Jesus was the Christ—the principle of revelation. They have said in their hearts that God does not reveal himself from heaven. Many people would be willing to accept the Mormon plan if they could eliminate the Joseph Smith story. But, of course, without that great manifestation there would be no church. We would be no different from any other church or organization, and without the principle of continuous revelation we would be in much the same condition. Without that principle the church of Christ cannot exist upon the earth. Not only does this principle pertain unto the leaders of the Church, but it pertains to all the sons and daughters of God.

It devolves upon us to gain the favor of God. Too frequently men and women are seeking the favor of their fellow creatures, and if they can obtain that to the extent that they will be exalted in the eyes of men, that is their ambition. Too frequently we are seeking the wealth of the world, thinking thereby to gain the favor of men. Yes, we may gain man's favor thereby but we cannot obtain the favor of God by devoting our thought and energy to the things of this world and neglecting the things of the spirit. We must be willing to give all that we have, and I cannot help but believe that someday when the books are opened and we stand before the great Judge, we shall find that some who have not made great impressions perhaps upon us, but who have been sincere and honest and have striven hard to live humbly before the Lord, will receive the greater rewards.

These men with whom I have been associated, and whose lives have been more or less an open book to the world, were men who had in their hearts first the kingdom of God, even though it meant not only the sacrifice of earthly wealth and the acclaim of their fellowmen, but ofttimes accepting and fulfilling assignments that were anything but desirable, that required a separation from their loved ones for long periods of time, and that involved the forsaking of ambitions and the endurance of what otherwise would have been very unhappy experiences. If one is to be a true follower of the Master, he must be willing to forsake all in order to do the Lord's work. He may have the peace of which the Master spoke shortly before leaving his disciples: "My peace I give unto you, not as the world giveth give I unto you. Let not your heart be troubled, neither let it be afraid."

He may also have the assurance that the Lord will

fulfill his promises, that he will leave him not alone, and that "whatsoever ye shall ask the Father in my name that is right, believing that ye shall receive, it shall be given unto you."

In perhaps the most glorious revelation given by the Lord to man regarding the exercise of the priesthood we read:

Behold, there are many called, but few are chosen. And why are they not chosen?

Because their hearts are set so much upon the things of this world, and aspire to the honors of men, that they do not learn this one lesson—

That the rights of the priesthood are inseparably connected with the powers of heaven, and that the powers of heaven cannot be controlled nor handled only upon the principles of righteousness.

That they may be conferred upon us, it is true; but when we undertake to cover our sins, or to gratify our pride, our vain ambition, or to exercise control or dominion or compulsion upon the souls of the children of men, in any degree of unrighteousness, behold, the heavens withdraw themselves; the Spirit of the Lord is grieved; and when it is withdrawn, Amen to the priesthood or the authority of that man. (D&C 121:34-37.)

So far as it is possible for men to conform their conduct to the law laid down by the Lord in the above scripture, these brethren of the General Authorities have endeavored to eliminate from their dispositions and from their conduct "pride, vain ambition," and they have avoided the exercise of "control or dominion or compulsion upon the souls of the children of men, in any degree of unrighteousness."

As mentioned at various times in this book, these men are not, nor do they claim to be, perfect men. They have been and are men of great ability, men of experience, and men of inspiration. But their ambitions and desires have been the welfare and progress of the Church, the righteous living of the members, and the strengthening of their testimonies; and their desire and supplication have been and are that the powers of heaven might be

subject only to their righteous desires. If conditions
otherwise have prevailed, I am sure that the Spirit
of the Lord was not pleased. My experience has
been such that I know of no such cases, although
it is possible that in individual instances such may
have occurred.

It is not only the General Authorities of the
Church, but the priesthood generally, who should
keep in mind the further instruction given:

No power or influence can or ought to be maintained by
virtue of the priesthood, only by persuasion, by long-suffering,
by gentleness and meekness and by love unfeigned;

By kindness, and pure knowledge, which shall greatly enlarge
the soul without hypocrisy, and without guile—

Reproving betimes with sharpness, when moved upon by
the Holy Ghost; and then showing forth afterwards an increase
of love toward him whom thou hast reproved, lest he esteem
thee to be his enemy;

That he may know that thy faithfulness is stronger than the
cords of death.

Let thy bowels also be full of charity towards all men, and
to the household of faith, and let virtue garnish thy thoughts
unceasingly; then shall thy confidence wax strong in the presence
of God; and the doctrine of the priesthood shall distil upon thy
soul as the dews from heaven.

The Holy Ghost shall be thy constant companion, and thy
scepter an unchanging scepter of righteousness and truth; and
thy dominion shall be an everlasting dominion, and without
compulsory means it shall flow unto thee forever and ever. (D&C
121:41-46.)

If all men in the Church could and would place
themselves in harmony with this instruction given
by the Lord, the time could not be far distant when
the Savior would come again and the reign of peace
would prevail upon the earth. Certainly that should
be our desire; that should be our goal; and that
time will eventually come. It contemplates the love
of God and the love of neighbor, of fellowman. It
contemplates a correct understanding of the priesthood and a determination to exercise it for the

benefit and blessing of mankind. By so doing, our
faith in God and his love for us will grow and increase. Our lives will be subject to the direction
and guidance of the Holy Ghost. The priesthood
will become what it was intended to become, the
power of God given to man to serve righteously
among his children.

God Moves in a Mysterious Way

I bear personal witness that God moves in a mysterious way, "his wonders to perform. He plants his
footsteps on the sea and rides upon the storm."

In his book *Stories of Latter-day Saints Hymns*
George D. Pyper gives the following regarding
William Cowper's writing of the hymn "God moves
in a Mysterious Way."

In the histories, biographies and memoirs of William Cowper,
examined by the writer, there is nothing to indicate just when
"God Moves in a Mysterious Way" was written. One story
related that "once upon a time" when he felt his weakness
coming on, he yielded to an impulse to drown himself in the
river Thames; that he called a cab and asked the cabman to
drive him to the river; that a heavy London fog suddenly gathered
and the cabman lost his way; that after driving aimlessly round
and round for some time, the cabman refused to continue and
ordered his passenger out; that Cowper stumbled to the walk
and found himself in front of his own door; that when he re-
covered his senses, he sat down and wrote "God Moves in a
Mysterious Way His Wonders to Perform." There is some justification
for the survival of this story. One writer said: He "had an intense
delusion that it was the Divine will for him . . . to drown himself, but the driver of the vehicle missed his way and Cowper was
diverted from his purpose." Then, too, Cowper's own memoirs
state that he was driven to the Thames with suicidal intent
but was prevented from carrying out his purpose by the appearance
of a wharf porter sitting on a pile of goods.

However, there is no doubt that the hymn was written in
view of his own dreadful experiences, and the hand of Providence
is plainly seen in preventing the consummation of an evil design.
The hymn was included in the Olvey Hymns . . . which were
published in 1787.

God Moves in a Mysterious Way

God moves in a mysterious way
His wonders to perform;
He plants his footsteps in the sea
And rides upon the storm.

Deep in unfathomable mines
Of never failing skill
He treasures up his bright designs
And works his sov'reign will.

Ye fearful Saints, fresh courage take;
The clouds ye so much dread
Are big with mercy and shall break
In blessings on your head.

Judge not the Lord by feeble sense,
But trust him for his grace;
Behind a frowning providence
He hides a smiling face.

His purposes will ripen fast,
Unfolding every hour;
The bud may have a bitter taste,
But sweet will be the flower.

Blind unbelief is sure to err
And scan his works in vain;
God is his own interpreter,
And he will make it plain.

It was the favorite song of Abraham Lincoln as well as of President Wilford Woodruff. When Brother Woodruff was president of the Church, at his request the council sang it more than any other.

We are finite; our Heavenly Father in infinite. His ways are not man's ways, and in many respects man would not understand them if they were made known to him. The apostle Paul said, "All things work together for the good of him that serves the Lord."

And in our day the Lord has said, "Search diligently, pray always, and be believing, and all things shall work together for your good, if ye walk uprightly and remember the covenant wherewith ye have covenanted one with another." (D&C 90:24.)

The prophet Lehi, in speaking to his son Jacob (2 Nephi 2), gave a discourse on the need for opposition in all things. He mentioned to him that he, Jacob, had suffered much sorrow and much affliction because of the rudeness of his brethren. Yet Lehi said, "Nevertheless, Jacob, my first-born in the wilderness, thou knowest the greatness of God, and he shall consecrate thine afflictions for thy gain."

He further said:

> For it must needs be, that there is an opposition in all things. If not so, . . . righteousness could not be brought to pass, neither wickedness, neither holiness nor misery, neither good nor bad.
>
> And if ye shall say there is no law, ye shall also say there is no sin. If ye shall say there is no sin, ye shall also say there is no righteousness. . . . And if there be no righteousness nor happiness there be no punishment nor misery. And if these things are not there is no God. And if there is no God we are not, neither the earth; for there could have been no creation of things, neither to act nor to be acted upon; wherefore, all things must have vanished away.
>
> And now, my sons, I speak unto you these things for your profit and learning; for there is a God, and he hath created all things, both the heavens and the earth, and all things that in them are, both things to act and things to be acted upon.
>
> And to bring about his eternal purposes in the end of man, after he had created our first parents, and the beasts of the field and the fowls of the air, and in fine, all things which are created, it must needs be that there was an opposition; even the forbidden fruit in opposition to the tree of life; the one being sweet and the other bitter.
>
> Wherefore, the Lord God gave unto man that he should act for himself, Wherefore, man could not act for himself save it should be that he was enticed by the one or the other. . . .
>
> But behold, all things have been done in the wisdom of him who knoweth all things.
>
> Adam fell that men might be; and men are, that they might have joy.

And the Messiah cometh in the fulness of time, that he may redeem the children of men from the fall. And because that they are redeemed from the fall they have become free forever, knowing good from evil; to act for themselves and not to be acted upon, save it be by the punishment of the law at the great and last day, according to the commandments which God hath given.

Wherefore, men are free according to the flesh; and all things are given them which are expedient unto man. And they are free to choose liberty and eternal life, through the great mediation of all men, or to choose captivity and power of the devil; for he seeketh that all men might be miserable like unto himself. (2 Nephi 2:11, 13-17, 24-27.)

Man naturally would prefer that misfortune, sickness, failure, and such things should pass him by, but if we had not trials or troubles, we could have no development, no progress, no faith, no salvation or exaltation.

The tree that stands to the windward side in the forest unprotected from other trees becomes firm and strong, and its roots sink deep into the soil that the tree may meet the onslaughts of the storm.

The man who has known no sickness or trouble cannot sympathize properly with the one who has met such trials. Severe sickness may be the ground from which the seed of faith sprouts and grows. Such things normally humble the person so suffering and draw him close to God, upon whom frequently he has no other reliance. What a joy comes into the heart of the individual who has proven to his own satisfaction that the Lord is with him through his Holy Spirit.

When the Lord decided to build an earth whereon we might dwell, he said, "And we will prove them herewith to see if they will do all things which the Lord their God shall command them." It was not merely to prove us, however, but that through the experiences of life, the proving yes, we might be made strong, we might be able to overcome and thereby become more and more like our Father, the Father of our spirits, that we might be "added upon," that we might be prepared to take on the responsibilities and blessings that would come through immortality and eternal life in our Father's kingdom.

This is a wonderful work. Those who have led this church have been blessed with the gift of faith and the inspiration and guidance of the Holy Spirit. Were this not the case, the Church could not have made the progress it has made. It is of the utmost importance that we learn to recognize the promptings of the Holy Spirit, and this, in a large measure, the leaders of the Church have learned in their positions, because they have had to rely upon the Lord and they have exercised faith in the Lord in the guidance of his Spirit. Were this not a fact, the Church could not have made the progress it has made. The work of the Lord would not have unfolded as it has done, and our Father's purposes would not have been accomplished. Mistakes would have been made very often, resulting in embarrassment and confusion to the Church.

The heavens were opened in the beginning of this dispensation through the faith of a boy. He asked in faith, "nothing wavering," and the Father and the Son appeared to him in answer to his humble but sincere prayer. Other heavenly messengers later came and gave their messages in response to the same power. The foundation of the Church was laid, and its principles and doctrines were given in response to the same kind of faith. The Lord is today making known his purposes in response to the faith of those who are called upon to preside over the Church and its destinies. This is the Lord's church; he is at the helm. The work of this dispensation, the dispensation of the fulness of times, must go on. The time is short, and if the work of this dispensation is to be accomplished, the Master, the Redeemer and Savior, must make known his will to his representatives here upon the earth. The work is speeding up and must of necessity do so in order that it may be completed in the desired time.

How important it is that every individual member should through prayer and faith obtain an unfaltering testimony of the gospel and so conduct his life that that faith may grow stronger day by day, doing nothing to displease the Lord, that his Spirit may not withdraw from him. If this were an accomplished fact, the knowledge of God would grow in the earth and the time of the Lord's second coming would be greatly hastened. As stated by Moroni, quoting the words of Christ, "If ye have faith, you can do all things which are expedient unto me."

EPILOGUE

It is a wonderful experience to have known and associated personally with the leaders of the Church, but it is impossible for me to do justice in the written word to the way I truly feel about these brethren. I can relate the experiences I have had with them, but I cannot portray in its proper light the spiritual warmth of President Grant or the conviction of his heart, his love of the gospel and his fellowmen.

I cannot describe as clearly as I should the love that President George Albert Smith had for mankind and for the Lord.

I cannot transmit to the reader the piercing look into one's eyes of President McKay. I cannot describe his affectionate handclasp, the music of his voice, or the full expression of his personality.

President Joseph Fielding Smith was a man who had deep insight pertaining to the meaning of the scriptures and the purpose of life. It is difficult by the written word to convey the depth of his soul and the sincerity of his love for his fellowmen.

President Harold B. Lee, a man of courage and decision, a great friend of mankind generally, with a depth of love and understanding of the gospel—it is not possible for me to portray in fullness on paper the picture that impresses me as I glance into the mirror of his soul.

We cannot too well place on paper or relate to our understanding the great influence that the Lord's Spirit had upon the Prophet Joseph Smith, or his influence upon his associates. The important thing is the person himself. Man is a son of God. For him the universe was created; there is a spark of divinity in his soul.

I think of the influence of the physician upon the sick person.

Man has inherited these traits, these virtues, these great possibilities and manifestations of his inheritance from his Heavenly Father.

These are the things that make our personalities and characters.

In my many years of service as secretary to the First Presidency of the Church, I have always felt that I was especially favored of the Lord—that, in fact, I had the best position in the Church, and in the world, for that matter. The brethren of the First Presidency and all of the General Authorities were and are special in my feelings, men whom the Lord has chosen and loves; men, as a matter of fact, whom he selected for his leaders before they were born because they have proven themselves before they came here and had the love and favor of our Heavenly Father because of their ability, their faith, their devotion to truth; men of leadership, dependability, and strength.

Normally men do not and should not seek these positions. As President Clark said on one occasion, "There is no career in the Church." He meant, of course, that working for the Church is not a means of advancing in church position. God's leaders are chosen by inspiration. It had never been my ambition to be a General Authority. I never considered myself belonging in that group of choice brethren. Over the years I have seen men thus chosen magnified and strengthened almost beyond imagination in helping their fellowmen and doing all in their power to build the kingdom of God.

That I should be chosen to be numbered with the General Authorities of the Church in my advanced years was a great surprise to me, but I know it to be a call from the Lord, and I recognize it as a great opportunity for service if I devote myself unselfishly to this work.

My heart is filled with gratitude for the privilege of visiting the various stakes of the Church, working with the leadership in these stakes, and partaking of their spirit as well as the spirit of the faithful Latter-day Saints with whom I come in contact. Each stake seems to have a personality of its own, but one recognizes the same spirit among the people wherever he goes.

It is a great responsibility to represent the Lord and his leaders in carrying the gospel message to the stakes and missions and endeavoring to inspire the people with a determination to serve the Lord, knowing that only by faithful, devoted service to our fellowmen can we achieve that goal which the Lord desires us to reach, namely, eternal life in our Father's kingdom. While great numbers of people come out to sacrament meetings, ward and stake activities, and stake conferences, and while wonderful meetings are held, one cannot do otherwise than feel sad that many people who have once had a testimony of the gospel have become careless and indifferent and are denying themselves the blessings that the Lord has promised the faithful.

I quote from a revelation given by the Lord through the Prophet Joseph at Harmony, Pennsylvania, in May 1829 to Joseph Knight: "And no one can assist in this work except he shall be humble and full of love, having faith, hope, and charity, being temperate in all things, whatsoever shall be entrusted to his care." (D&C 12:8.)

In my own feelings I am satisfied that my love for the brethren has greatly increased, as has also my appreciation for the leadership of this church in the stakes and missions. My faith in the membership has been enlarged, and I know beyond any question that this work will go forward and accomplish the great mission for which it was established.

INDEX